**Learn How To Win**

# So You Wanna Be A GAMBLER?

## By John Patrick
Professional Gambler

## SLOTS — ROULETTE

- Bankroll
  - Knowledge of the Game
    - Money Management
      - Discipline

# DEDICATION

*To my Mother and my Father.*

*To my daughters Lori and Colleen.*

*How I love these four people!*

# ACKNOWLEDGEMENTS

I would like to give my sincere thanks to the people who assisted in the completion of this book. Their contributions come in the form of intelligent input in the areas of gambling theories.

First, there is my partner, Ted Butner. His knowledge of casino games and money management is unmatched.

Thanks go to Diane and John Guibas, who operate one of my schools in Jamaica Hills, New York. (212-526-6167) John is an expert card counter, with excellent theories.

Finally, my thanks go to the finest group of instructors in the country. These professionals have no equals in their ability to play and teach: Les Scally, Jeff Dalia, Carl Bajor, Irv Hyatt, Bart Parodi, Greg Lantz, Austin Kosik, Tony Satus, Mike Schreck, Howie Goldstein, Mark Zimmer, Ron Ludden, Paul Foreman, Jack Klarman, Jim Gilrain, Charles Zimmerman and Bob Nash.

All of these people are experts, and it is my privilege to work with, and learn from them.

# PREFACE

*So You Wanna Be A Gambler* is a book about slots and roulette. It contains money management systems and theories on discipline.

I'm not going to be able to stop you from playing the slots and I'm not even interested in trying. But, if you follow the money management systems laid out for you, it'll change your whole outlook on that endeavor. It's called winning and walking.

The roulette systems are controlled methods, by which you can play comfortably with the knowledge that your chances of losing have been minimized.

I will teach you how to win, and that's not an easy chore, based on the way most people play. But win you will.

If you want to take an intelligent approach to slots and roulette, read "So You Wanna Be A Gambler". You'll enjoy it. But most of all you'll see how a strict system of money management and discipline can change your approach to gambling.

# CONTENTS

## KNOWLEDGE OF THE GAME - ROULETTE

## MONEY MANAGEMENT

# DISCIPLINE

# ODDS AND ENDS

# INTRODUCTION TO GAMBLING  1

## So You Wanna Be A Gambler?

Obviously, if you're reading a book on gambling, I have to assume that you would like to know something about the subject. Well, this book will cover certain aspects of the worlds of gambling — in this case the games of roulette and slot machines.

Before we get into the games themselves, let's go right to the heart of all people who gamble. In fact, if we take all of the people who gamble on football, baseball, or basketball games; or play poker, gin-rummy, pinochle, or bingo; or visit any of the casinos in Nevada or Atlantic City; or try their hand at craps, blackjack, roulette, slot machines, or baccarat, we would cover quite a few men and women. For kicks, I'll throw in the thousands of people who frequent the race tracks in New York, New Jersey, California and Florida, both flats and harness. We add a few million daily bingo players, and touch it off with the multi-million daily wagers on the weekly, monthly, and daily lotteries, and you can see that a majority of the populace is involved in some type of gambling every week. In fact, gambling is probably the second most popular activity undertaken by people all the time. Just think about it. These opportunities are placed in front of people every day. They are tempted to take a chance at winning money which they need. And, once people get a taste of betting, they're bitten. The gambling bug takes a strong hold on their priorities.

Many, many senior citizens spend their nights around local bingo games. Watch them entering the hall laughing, anticipating victory, hoping and praying that this is the night. They search through hundreds of cards looking for lucky numbers, birthdates, license plates, or match-ups; anything that will give them the money they want. . . and need.

As the night wears on and your cards turn up nothing but losses, you become anxious, disgusted, surly, and irritated. Finally, it's over. This action that you looked forward to has come to a close and a frustrating one at that. You never even came close. The cranky looks on these people's faces as they leave make it all so clear as to who the winners and losers are.

I've watched these people, mostly women and the majority of them being senior citizens, play bingo. It is rarely handled like a night out. It is approached as a way to make money. To gamble. Just think of all your relatives, friends, neighbors, acquaintances, and all of the other people who partake of some type of gambling every day.

See if this story doesn't strike a personal note. It is not an isolated example. The story could be applied to anyone who takes on any of the gambling games. Hope, anticipation, confidence, cockiness, despair, frustration, anger, disgust all come into play. You know what is missing? Something they all fail to realize. Reality! Since most people lose at gambling, and eventually get knocked off that dream-cloud world, they are shocked back to reality by the fact that they have again lost.

You know why they lose? Because they don't know how to win. I didn't say they didn't know how to play. I said how to win. That, in itself, is an art. This will be discussed at greater length later on, but for now, remember what I said: "They don't know *how* to win."

Why do people gamble? There are many reasons, but I'll name just a few.

a)    Need
b)    Challenge
c)    Excitement
d)    Pastime

*Need.* This, in my humble opinion, is far and away the primary reason that people gamble. They need the money. They need extra money for the special things that they want to provide for the family. Or, they need the money for a stack of bills or to go on vacation. This need for money is what I believe drives most people to gamble.

*Challenge.* Ah, yes, the ever present challenge. The high roller who does not need money enjoys the challenge. He loves the thought of attacking the crap table or blackjack pit or even breaking the bank at poker. I don't believe he is playing to win as his primary goal. I think the challenge of the chase is more enticing. Who's to say he is right or wrong?

*Excitement.* You can just feel it. Ever walk into a casino at the start of a three day vacation and hear the whirl of the slot machines, the chatter at the crap tables, and the general electric in the air? Or, how about the start of a horse race? The horses approach the starting gate and the buzzing starts. The crowd moves toward the fence and the air is filled with excitement. Whether you've bet $2 or $200, it is there. If you've ever been to a track, you'll know of what I speak. Gambling is exciting.

*Pastime.* I think so. I think people love to spend a day at the track, in a casino, or sitting in front of a TV set and bet on the game of the day — whatever it is. I believe many people look forward to the weekly poker game or even to the "pots" at the nightly bowling leagues.

In other words, any and all of these reasons could be applied to most everyone who gambles. And why not? Gambling is every bit a part of our lives as it is to people all over the world.

I am not disputing it. I am only trying to make a point. If, in fact, it is such an integral part of so many people's existence, why don't they learn how to win?

So You Wanna Be A Gambler? Good, but do it intelligently. That's what I'll be harping on.

# INTRODUCTION TO GAMBLING  2

## Two Different Games

Let me give you an idea of what you can expect in this book. I will discuss the games of Roulette and Slot Machines. The games offer varying degrees of possible success. The chances of winning are as follows:

a)  Roulette———Fair on inside bets; Good on outside bets

b)  Slots ————Lousy

But you want to know something? There are millions of people today who still try to conquer the one-armed bandits. And yet, these same millions of people have never ventured into the Baccarat pit, picked up a set of dice, or played a hand of blackjack —the three games in a casino that offer you a chance of winning. Why? They're scared. They're in awe of these games. They never learned how to play them. They think you have to be a genius plus to compete. They also feel that those games are too hard to learn. They're wrong right down the line.

I cover these games in other books I have written, all under the same title of "So You Wanna Be A Gambler". In this book you will learn how to suc-cessfully compete at the Roulette table and how, if you must, play a little slots. Maybe I can convert some of you to the proper way of gambling. That merely means, "Learning how to win".

The game of Roulette is strictly in the category of "fairly good chance of winning". This is so because of the En Prison Rule that is used in Atlantic City casinos. This rule is in force in a few Las Vegas houses, and definitely reduces the clout that the casinos hold over the novice. This rule has reduced the players' chances of losing and has transformed a sucker game into a fairly variable encounter. In gambling, you must learn to minimize your losses by playing in low vig games, and this rule does help.

I'm not telling you to rush down and play this game, but I'm also not telling you to completely ignore it.

But let's get one thing straight right off the bat. If you don't know "how to win", you're wasting your time at any type of gambling. That is the difference between the novice and the pro. One is a dummy. The other an expert. You place yourself in whatever category you think you belong. Then digest the information laid out in these chapters, and let me know what your personal classification is.

Gambling is a serious business. And in case you're not aware of it yet, it is also an expensive undertaking. If you like to lose or if it doesn't bother you, nothing I say is going to make a difference. So set your mind now. You either want to learn how to win or accept the fact you'll be considered a "mark". (That's a dummy.)

You can learn all there is to know about a certain game, but if you can't manage your money you will never become a winner. Besides covering the two games, I will also harp on that all important facet of gambling, money management, and the old equalizer, Discipline. I expect you to digest all of the information on Discipline. It is the wall that separates the pros from the novice. Once you break down that wall, winning will become as entertaining as eating. Naturally, you will not win all of the time. That is impossible. But you will lessen your losses, and when your winning days do come, you will find how easy it is to win and walk.

Why would I write a book that covers the games of Roulette and Slot Machines? You've probably already figured out the answer. Because, no matter how much you tell a person about avoiding games like Roulette, and Slot Machines, and Big Wheel, they still are attracted to these games to try their luck.

I am not condemning roulette since the casinos in Atlantic City have done a terrific job of reducing your chances of losing at this game by adding the en prison rule to their tables. Also, the casinos in Las Vegas offer the game of roulette with very, very small minimums in effect. That allows people with short bankrolls to be able to compete. Well, I'll show you how. The rest is up to you. But don't discount these low minimum requirements that Nevada casinos are offering. They allow you to stay in the game.

As for the slot machines, they have been around for decades and will always be found in gambling houses. Their drawing power is astonishing. People are just drawn to these machines by the thousands.

The attraction value of the slots blends into the casinos like warm butter into a plate of hot potatoes. Take away the slots, and you damage the overall image of casino life. Most everyone who enters the casinos takes a flyer at these machines. What I will do is merely alert you as to what you are up against. Whether you decide to play these machines or not is strictly up to you.

Can you imagine how a guy who visits the track every day would feel towards me if I told him that he is not supposed to bet on the ponies?

How about Florence and Josephine, constant visitors to the Happy Hour Bingo game every night. If I told them not to attend these Bingo gatherings, there would be a lynch mob get together on my front lawn. No, I am not intent on discouraging your choice of gambling outlets. I will merely make you aware of the proper way to attack the game of your choice.

Will you listen to what I have to say during the course of these chapters? Some will; some won't.

If I tell you what you want to hear, you will be receptive. But the important facets, like money management and discipline, are very hard to acquire. That is where I will lose some hearty souls.

Learning *how* to win is difficult. Everyone can't do it. But, I honestly hope you consider what I have to say. Who knows, you may become a winner and enjoy it.

# INTRODUCTION TO GAMBLING    3

## Vigorish In Gambling

Do you know what vigorish is? You don't? Well then, you'd better digest this chapter. Because vigorish is the gun at your head, the knife in your back, and the noose around your neck.

It's the difference, baby. The edge that the house holds over all gamblers. It's the vigorish, or vig as I will call it that decides how quickly you will lose.

In every game that you make a wager on, that ever present vig will be present. Most times you can't even see it, but it's there just the same.

Professional gamblers will only play in games that have a small edge or vig to the house. The novice, since he doesn't understand vigorish, will play any game completely oblivious to the power of this three-letter word.

There has to be a vig attached to every game. How else could the house pay for the lights, drinks, rent, salaries, etc. If all games were played on an even basis, the house would then be in a position of gambling as to whether they would win or lose. And, casinos don't gamble. Neither do race tracks or state-run lotteries. People gamble, and buck the vig of the house.

The important thing is to find out which games

have the smallest vig applied to it and then play that game...PERFECTLY.

First, let's give you an idea of what affect a vig has on a bet. We'll take a football game between the Dallas Cowboys and the Green Bay Packers. Let's assume the Packers are visiting Dallas on a Sunday afternoon and the official line shows that the Cowboys are favored to win by seven points.

That means if you bet on Dallas you must give seven points, and if you bet on Green Bay you will receive seven points. In the opinion of the line-maker in Las Vegas, this seven-point spread makes it an even game.

You call your local bookie to place your bet. Suppose you wish to bet enough to win $50. In gambling terms, this is called a ten timer — each $5 increment being considered a 'time'. If you wanted a five timer, you would be trying to win $25, and so on.

Suppose Mr. A wants to bet on Dallas. He tells his bookie he wants the Dallas Cowboys, minus seven points, ten times. Now the bookie has overhead to meet, too. So, if Mr. A wants to bet $50 he must pay a vig of $5, or 10%, for the right to make his bet. He must risk $55 to win $50. That extra $5 is the vig he is fighting.

After Mr. A places his $55 to $50 wager, Mr. B calls the same bookie, only he wants to bet on Green Bay. He announces: "Give me Green Bay plus the 7 points, 10 times". He, in turn, risks $55 to win $50. The bookie's work sheet looks like this:

Mr. A — —     Dallas minus 7          55 to 50
Mr. B — —     Green Bay plus 7       55 to 50

Let's assume Dallas wins the game 28 to 7. The bookie pays Mr. A $50, and collects $55 from Mr. B. He was in a no-lose situation. The $5 he was sure to win, regardless of which team won, is his vigorish. Naturally, you only pay it if you lose. If Green Bay had won, Mr. B would have collected $50, and Mr. A would have paid $55. The bookie tries to get his "action" to match so that he is sure of collecting, regardless of who wins.

The same is true of every game you play. The operator must charge this vig to stay in business. Your responsibility is to find games that offer low percentages against you, and play only those games. Otherwise, the vigorish will grind you out.

Moving over to the game of roulette, you get another easy idea of what percentage you are fighting at the table. The layout in roulette shows that you can bet on any number from 1 through 36, and also 0 and 00. That gives the house 38 different chances for that little ball to drop into a particular slot. Suppose you put a $1 chip on number 8. If number 8 wins, the house will pay you 35-1. You get your original dollar back, and also $35 in winnings.

Examine your chances of winning. When you placed your dollar on number 8, you had one chance of winning, and 37 chances of losing. That's because that little ball could have dropped into any one of 37 other slots besides number 8. Your chances of winning are 37 to 1 against you. The house pays you 35 to 1 if you win. The difference between what they should pay you, (37-1), and what they do pay, (35-1), is called vigorish.

In this case, the vig is 5.26%. Every time you play

a number straight up on the roulette board, corners, splits, lines, or streets, you are fighting 5.26% against you.

Now you have an idea of what vigorish is all about. The house is entitled to this percentage. Like I've said, your job is to take them on when you have the least chance of losing. Will you do this? I rather doubt it. Most people are just too plain lazy to go to all of this "trouble" to find these low vig games. That's when you get the label of "fish". You deserve it.

Since I am talking about casino games, I will list the vig, or percentage against you, when you step up to a table.

1) **ROULETTE**— —5.26%. Except, in the case of the line bet that includes 0—00—1—2—3. In this case, the vig against you is 7.19.

2) **BIG WHEEL**— —16.67%. Did that register in the back of your mind? 16.67%—that's some belt in the gut.

3) **SLOT MACHINES**— —In N.J., anywhere from 13% to 17%. State laws require that each machine must repay 87% of money wagered. Again, a shot to the gut. In Vegas, there are machines that return as much as 95%, a fair enough figure, for those with no knowledge of other games.

4) **BACCARAT**— —1.17% if you play the Bank, and 1.38% if you play Player. Obviously, the house is providing a game where their clout is not too heavy. Have you played Baccarat recently? It's a great game.

5) **CRAPS**— —Eight tenths of one percent. That is, if

you play the Pass or Don't Pass Lines and take the true odds. By playing the place bets and placing the six and/or eight, your vig is only 1.51%. Each bet has a different vig, but the opportunity is there to make plays that don't whack your starting bankroll.

6) **BLACKJACK** — —1.5%, if you're a perfect Basic Strategy player. But, the worse you perform in your knowledge of basic strategy, the higher the vig gets against you. A dumb player could be bucking percentages of 30% to 40% against him.

The Card Counter in Blackjack — I mean the real card counter, not a person who has an idea of what card counting is all about — has about a 2% edge on the house. Brother, that's some edge.

Obviously, the best games to play are Blackjack, Craps, and Baccarat. If you really want to get serious, become a card counter. These games offer the least amounts of vigorish pounding against you. But will that stop people from playing the other games? Of course not. But when you're finished with this book, I'm sure you will have a stronger awareness of what you're up against. You'd better be aware...

# 4  INTRODUCTION TO GAMBLING

## The Novice

There are two types of people who go into a casino; experts and dummies. An expert plays games that offer him the least chance of losing. He is an expert in the game or games he plays. He practices the art of money management, and he possesses the most important virtue of all; discipline. He is an expert, and he usually wins.

And then, there is the dummy. He is the opposite of all of the above. The casinos love the dummy. They know that it is only a matter of time before their foolish play and haphazard money management causes them to go broke. How about you? Are you an expert or a dummy?

I'm not trying to be insulting. I am trying to make you realize that gambling is a rough business. Unless you're prepared to do battle in a rough enterprise, you shouldn't be there.

Let's tone down my description of the lousy player. I will refer to him as a novice. A novice is a beginner. For instance, a person takes up golf and is given the description of being a novice. There is no disgrace there. Anyone who is starting out should be considered a novice. After they've played a few years, naturally, their game improves and they are no longer considered beginners.

Let's take the gambler. When they start out, they are considered novices. Naturally, after a couple of years of gambling, they learn how to bet and are becoming quite adept at winning. They become perfect players based on the constant attention they give to the games of their choice.

No one should even throw a pair of dice unless they know the game inside out. And just as surely, no one should sit at a blackjack table and risk their money on a game that rough unless they were perfect. Only a dummy would do that.

And that brings us back to question one. Are you a novice? How long have you been playing blackjack, craps, or poker? How often do you bet on football and baseball games? How often do you go the track???

Are you perfect at the game you undertake? If you're not, then why do you play? Give me a good reason why you play. Not a dopey answer like, "But I enjoy it", — —you must be nuts. You must be a _____ .

I am trying to make a point — a very important point. If you don't understand every single facet of the game you are betting on, there is no way you should risk your money.

In a capsule, the expert has an excellent chance of winning.

The novice has little or no chance of winning.

Examine your approach to gambling. If you're a novice, learn the game of your choice. You'll never be called a _____ again.

# 5 INTRODUCTION TO GAMBLING

## Do Casinos Cheat?

Let's face it, you've heard that question hundreds of times. I know I have. A lot of people feel that since the casinos win so often, surely it is a logical assumption.

Are you kidding me? Of course the casinos don't cheat — not at all. How I hate it when someone goes to the table, loses $400 and then starts complaining that the game was fixed. It wasn't fixed. He probably lost because he didn't know how to play. I've also read some books where the author wastes page after page complaining about cheating dealers, cheating casinos, and a lot of bull about watching for these things.

Most people who gamble don't have a full awareness of how to even play, and now you're asking for them to look for cheating? Pure nonsense.

Let's go back for a second to the cry-baby who lost the $400. Why did he wait until he lost $400 to start bellowing about cheating? Are we to believe that he didn't know they were cheating until his last $5 bet? Otherwise, why would he stay at the table if he knew he was being cheated?

You see how silly it sounds about cheating? Don't

think the "cries of cheat" ring out only in the casinos. I've heard the same belly aching at race tracks, in poker games, and after-sporting events such as football, baseball, and basketball. I say it's pure nonsense.

One final observation. Would you please tell me why the casinos would want to take a chance at cheating when the majority of players are so bad? They need to cheat as bad as I need a second head. Why kill the golden goose?

The casinos don't cheat. It is the stupid players and lack of discipline by the patrons that cause people to lose.

# 6   INTRODUCTION TO GAMBLING

## The Big Four

Do not skip this chapter. Digest what I am saying. To win in casinos, at the race tracks, at cards, or sports betting you need four things:

1. Bankroll
2. Knowledge of the Game
3. Money Management
4. Discipline

That's it! That the Big Four. Without it, you cannot win. With 75% of it you won't win consistently. You need the Big Four every single time you bet. If you read my book on blackjack, entitled *So You Wanna Be A Gambler,* you will know how strongly I feel on this subject. If you perfect a system based on this theory, you will learn how to win at gambling.

A section will be devoted to each of the above, but for now, I would like to merely let you know what each category stands for.

**BANKROLL.** It's the beginning; the start of your war against the casino. The amount of money you take to the casino is your bankroll. It doesn't have to be $7,000, $2,000, or even $700. Your bankroll is your own private business. But, whatever the amount, that is what dictates how much you can win or lose on a given day. After you decide on the amount of money you are taking to the casino, all decisions of reward and loss are pre-determined. This is covered in detail in "Bankroll — the Beginning".

**KNOWLEDGE OF THE GAME.** It is imperative that you know everything there is to know about the game you intend to play. Being very good is not good enough. Being perfect is required. Am I being too harsh on you?

Let's go back to the chapter on vigorish. You'll notice that the blackjack player, who is an expert in basic strategy, is fighting only a 1½% edge to the house. He knows exactly what moves to make for every hand he has, based on the dealer's up card. That means even being perfect, his chance of winning is still only 50-50.

Are you getting the point? If the perfect player has only a 50-50 chance, why be anything less? You'll only lose quicker and more often if you are weak at the game you play. It is so easy to perfect the game you wish to gamble on. Yet, only about 5% of all the people who gamble know everything about the game they challenge. No wonder there is such a large percentage of losers.

How about you? Are you perfect? If not, quit. You're wasting your time and money.

**MONEY MANAGEMENT.** How you manage the money you bring to a casino is called money management. So what if you have a large bankroll. If you can't manage it or don't know how to bet, you're spinning your wheels. I'll show you money management. You want to follow it? Good! If not, it's only a matter of time until you're beaten.

**DISCIPLINE.** The ball game! This is what destroys the novice in a casino. A complete lack of discipline. I'll cover this category in detail later on. Will you adhere to the rules I lay out for you? Nope!!! Because you'd rather play than learn how to win.

There you have the Big Four. A simple formula for success. If you master it, you'll be a consistent winner. It's up to you.

# INTRODUCTION TO GAMBLING

# 7

## The Little Three

The Big Four is a necessity. I'm going to give you a little something extra to put in your bonnet. Something to be aware of when you get involved in gambling. I call it the Little Three simply for the purpose of keeping it apart from the Big Four. Here they are:

1. LOGIC
2. THEORY
3. TRENDS

**LOGIC.** In gambling, everything has a logical explanation. There is no mystery to anything connected to a game of chance. You don't need a college education or a master's degree to play. You don't even need a grade school diploma. Anyone can gamble as long as they have the bread.

Yet, I hear so many people complain, "I don't understand that game", or, "That's too complicated for me". Oh, they bet on these games even though they don't understand them. Why should they go to all that trouble to learn how to win??? Dopes—that's what they are. They're too stupid to realize that they could cut their losses down to the barest minimums by learning how to win.

Every single move that is required in a given game has a logical explanation. A professional gambler is an expert in the games he plays. That's why he is able to compete. A surgeon is an expert in medicine and qualified to perform an operation. Simply, because he knows his business. You wouldn't want the gambler to perform an appendectomy on you. That isn't a logical move. Nor, is it logical for a doctor with all his knowledge in medicine to sit in a poker or gambling game and know nothing about what is going on or what is the best percentage move to make, and risk his money on the outcome.

And, yes, this example is relative. It's just that people treat gambling like it was a lark. It isn't. It's a rough business and a big reason why many people go broke. Learn the logical move to make. It'll turn out to be the best move.

**THEORY.** Theory is actually an opinion. It is never wrong. When a person is an expert at a given endeavor, how he or she uses that knowledge is their opinion or theory as to how to put that knowledge to its greatest use.

Let's take two different basketball coaches. Both are excellent players and successful college coaches. They know the game of basketball inside and out and are considered experts in their field.

One coach's theory as to how to play defense is man to man. The other coach opts for a zone defense. Both coaches have exployed two different theories down through the years, regardless of the type of personnel they have. Tall, short, fast, or slow they teach their players how to adjust to the type of defense that they believe works the best.

Both are succcessful. Yet, both use different theories as to how they teach the same subject. Neither one is wrong in their own individual approach.

The same is true in gambling. When you learn how to play, I want you to perfect your own theory. Naturally, you will not buck obvious poor percentage moves. What you will do is acquire a strong opinion on the way to get the best use out of your knowledge.

Theory—give it some thought.

**TRENDS.** In gambling, trends dominate. When a pattern develops in an even confrontation it tends to stay that way for periods of time. They're called streaks. I can't explain the reasons why this happens because I don't know. Let's take the example of flipping a coin. There are only two decisions that can be reached. It will end up heads or tails. That's all. It is a 50-50 proposition as to which will occur each time the coin is flipped. Just because there are only two decisions that could occur, it does not mean that the results will end up in an even pattern of heads/tails/heads/tails/heads, etc. It probably will happen that somewhere down the road after thousands or millions of flips the results will equal out, and there will be the same number of heads and tails.

That does not mean that the decisions will alternate in a system. It is more likely that you will get 4, 5, 6, 7, 8 heads in a row and then a streak of tails. Try it sometime. Notice how a trend of one side and then the other will appear.

I always marvel at the people at a roulette table who stand and watch that little ball fall into one of the slots. Let's say 8, black. On the next spin it shows 2, black. Right away they rush to make a bet on red because they think red is 'due' to come because black has shown twice in a row.

That is an illogical assumption. The ball surely doesn't know what has occurred on the previous decision. The chances of red or black appearing on subsequent spins is still 50-50. Become aware of this trend syndrome that has a habit of popping up in even proposition situations. In layman's terms, whenever you are involved in a game of chance, and the vigorish against you is very small, look for streaks to come. If one side wins, look for a repeat of that side rather than trying to outguess the dice, cards, or team by betting on the opposite side for no other reason than that it lost the previous decision.

Naturally, there will be times when a chopping pattern will develop, such as black/red/black/red/black in roulette. So what? Anything is possible in gambling. I am only trying to make you aware that this chopping trend will not happen habitiously. Streaks will dominate.

How long is a streak? It could be six, five, four, or two in a row. Do you think it is easy to win three hands in a row in blackjack? It is not. If you were to walk up to a table, be the best card-counter in the country, and ask for odds on winning three consecutive hands, the house would have to lay you 7 to 1. That is your chance of winning three straight hands. Wouldn't you say that you are at a slight disadvantage? Well, you are. Yet, people play so aggressively that they look to win six, seven, eight hands in a row. Ridiculous! That's hard. You must be aware of streaks, but at the same time you must be cognizant of the fact that it is very difficult to get long streaks. My money management will show you how to take advantage of both the long and short ones.

There you have the Little Three. They are not as dominant a necessity as the Big Four, but you'd darn well better know what they're about.

This concludes our introduction to gambling. Remember, I am not condoning the fact that you wish to invest your money in a game of chance. Nor, am I condemning you for doing the same. My objective is to make you aware of what you are up against in the casino. You must realize that when you are perfect at the game of your choice, your chances of winning are only 50-50. So, it behooves you to become perfect in the game you pick and then money management will have a chance to work.

# 1    BANKROLL

## Bankroll — The Beginning

This is the start. The bankroll is your compass. Every single, solitary bet you make is based on that bankroll. It gives you the direction for your every move in gambling. You decide on how much money you're going to take with you and the ground work is then laid out as to which type table you approach — either $10, $5, $3, etc.

The decision as to how much money you will win or lose has also been determined by that bankroll. This is because any person with an ounce of intelligence would never make a trip to a casino without setting a win goal or a loss limit.

Take yourself, for example. I know you're a person with both feet on the ground. You've got a good job, beautiful family, a few dollars in the bank, and a couple hundred dollars hidden in a shoe in the closet. That's your gambling money. You only use it when you sneak down to the casino for an afternoon of gambling.

Being an intelligent person, you set a goal for yourself. You decide ahead of time exactly how much money you would like to win on that particular day. At the same time, you set what is called a "Loss Limit". In no way, shape, or form will you lose more than this set amount. I know darn well that a sharp person like you has set these percentages ahead of time.

To be sure, you're not like I.M. Pinhedd, your next door neighbor. He goes to the casino with $200 and dreams of winning $10,000. He'll play until the $200 is gone or the casino is broke. He has no intelligent goal in mind. Only a desire to keep right on betting until it's time to leave. He could turn that $200 into $800, but that's not enough. In fact, no amount is enough.

The same is true when he is losing. Do you think he sets a limit on how much of his bankroll he will lose? Of course not. He'll bet right down to his last $1 chip and then start throwing loose change on the table, hoping to scrape up enough to make a final bet.

This jerk has no more of an idea as to how to set a loss limit than he knows how to spell win goal. He goes with a short bankroll and flounders all day long until he is mercifully saved by the fact that the bus is leaving or his vacation is over.

Now I know that you're not like the Pinhedds of the world. You would never be so stupid as to ever make a series of bets without initially setting goals for yourself as to how much you would like to win; and, just as importantly, to set loss limits which would signal your end to betting for the day.

There is no set figure that a bankroll has to match. Bankroll is your own personal starting block. If that amount is $2000 or $200, it still constitutes a bankroll. Most peoples' problems stem from the fact that they do not know how to handle their bankroll.

A guy with $200 is actually "playing short". He doesn't have a strong starting amount. After he loses a few bets, the money he has left dwindles a bit, and now he becomes panicky. He starts making illogical moves with his bets, as he is scared that a few more losses will result in his going broke. That's where the term 'scared money' comes into play. A guy in a losing streak starts adjusting that remaining amount of money — trying to make it last.

Let me lay some cards right on the table. Millions of people gamble. And, most of them are dummies. They do not know how to win. I did *NOT* say they didn't know how to *PLAY.* I said they didn't know how to *WIN.* That's a super, gigantic difference. Do you know why people don't know how to win? They have a simple, little malady known as stupidity.

This disease is prevalent in most people who gamble. Again, it is not reflected in their knowledge of the game, but in their actions after they get ahead. That's when stupidity takes over. Instead of accepting a win percentage, these geniuses fall victim to another common problem called "greeditus". Do you have it? Be honest. If you do, don't worry. It's curable. The medicine is hard to swallow, but it does work.

Ok, let's go back to square one. Where do you begin in gambling? Bankroll!!! It is the first part of the Big Four. It is the beginning.

# BANKROLL

## How Much Is A Bankroll?

How much should you take to a casino? A good question. Actually, you never have enough. For some reason, people think that the few dollars they set aside to wager gives them the right to look for returns of double and triple their investment.

It's amazing that for the millions of people who gamble, so many of them have a definite lack of insight into the proper way to bet.

Tip #1. Decide on your bankroll, regardless of how much it is. Five thousand dollars is a bankroll. So is one thousand. So is five hundred. So is $200. Got the point? There is no set amount. You must learn to base your decisions on the amount you have.

If you can afford to bring only $300 to the table, then don't expect a king's ransom as your profit. Be happy with whatever profit you can derive from that money.

Where do you decide on that return? Outside the casino. When you leave your house in the morning, you're well aware of how much money you have in your sock. Make your decisions right then and there. In all honesty, you should never gamble with short or scared money. It affects your method of play, your concentration, and your entire approach to gambling.

Think of the times you went to Las Vegas or Atlantic City with a short bankroll. Let's say, $200. Now, that $200 means a great deal to you within the confines of your own personal life. But, matched against the odds of casino games, it is pale by comparison.

If you could maintain the same respect you have for that $200 after you enter the casino just as you respect it in your personal life, you would take a giant stride in learning how to win!

But, no, the aura of that casino engulfs you. All possibilities for rationale are quickly swept away. When you get ahead, it is never enough. When you fall behind, you use the balance of your money to try and recoup the losses. If you could but understand the true value of your bankroll and the exact amount of its' pulling power, you would become a sensible bettor. I, personally, am a conservative bettor. I believe that most professional gamblers are more conservative than aggressive. But, you can be sure that they all have bankrolls to work with. Naturally, when they lose that bankroll, the party is over. That's true for anyone. If you don't have the bread, you can't compete.

I have theories as to how to control a bankroll, and, since they work, I stay with them. First off, I set an amount of money I would accept as my win goal for a given day. That is my Win Goal. Next, I have a limit that I place on my bankroll that is never exceeded if I start to lose. That is called my Loss Limit.

In the next chapter, I will detail these figures. But, for now, realize how important these predetermined percentages are.

Next, based on my bankroll, I set minimums on the table where I hope to compete. For instance in blackjack, I want at least 30 times the amount of the table minimum before I will play. At a $5 table, I must have at least $150 or 30 times 5 to play with. At a $10 table, it is 30 × 10, or $300. And so on. This guarantees that I will never be playing with scared money.

When you reach the sections on money management, you will see how the bankroll is divided into sessions. But for now, just concentrate on the bankroll.

Let's say you want to play roulette. You can't comfortably play with a handfull of $1 chips and honestly expect to stay alive for a period of time. One or two losing spins of the wheel and your short bankroll will cause gray hair to sprout on your cranium. You'll curse your luck, give dirty looks to the croupier, and demand that the wheel be checked for inbalance.

It's not the wheel that's out of whack; it's your thinking. If you had the proper bankroll, you wouldn't have to sweat out a few losses. You'd be able to shake them off and play comfortably. Before you gamble, get a good starting bankroll. It's the beginning of the war and you need the ammunition.

# 3 BANKROLL

## Loss Limits

I've already told you that the bankroll you bring to battle is your own personal decision. How you handle it is elaborated on in the chapters on money management. But for now, I want you to study the bankroll you will be using.

Don't be embarrassed by the size of your stake. If you're at a table and the guy next to you is betting hundred dollar chips, so what? It's none of your business; and besides, you should be concentrating on the game at hand and not checking the customers.

I'm not concerned with what you bring with you, only that you know how to control it. Remember what I said about accepting your bankroll? I've got a scoop for you. There's nothing you can do about the size of the money you are 'forced' to start with. If your economic situation is such that $300 is all you can scrape together, then let's concentrate on that figure and forget about crying crocodile tears over your shortage of funds.

Before you step into that battlefield, you must take stock of your situation. First off, you set a Loss Limit. This is done by setting a percentage of your bankroll that you will lose before running up the white flag. I have strong theories (Little Three) about these percentages, and follow them religiously. I set limits that I will not exceed when I enter a casino. This does not mean I absolutely, positively have to play exactly to that limit. But it does mean I cannot exceed it.

For instance, in roulette my loss limit is 50%. I cannot lose more than 50% of what I start with. I could lose 35% on a given day and still quit if I see the trends (Little Three) going constantly against me. Why fight a losing battle? But I will not lose a dollar more than the maximum loss limit which is 50%. Everyone should have these limits to go by; otherwise, you have lost control of your money situation.

Following is the Loss Limits I place on all Casino games:

a)  Craps . . . . . . . . . . . . . . . . . . . . . . . . . .50%
b)  Blackjack . . . . . . . . . . . . . . . . . . . . .40%
c)  Baccarat . . . . . . . . . . . . . . . . . . . . . .50%
d)  Roulette . . . . . . . . . . . . . . . . . . . . . .50%
e)  Slots (if you must play) . . . . . . . . . . .10%

When you lose the percentage of your starting bankroll, as stated above, you are done for the day. You are finished betting, regardless of how much longer you wanted to play. It doesn't matter if you feel lucky, if somebody begs you to keep playing, if the bus isn't leaving for another four hours, if your junket has twelve more hours to last before you leave Vegas for another six months, or any other such ridiculous nonsense. Your gambling for that day is over.

Now you're dying to tell me that if you're only going to lose half of your $300 why not just bring $150 with you? This is a psychological move. Remember what I stressed right from the beginning—*Learn* how to win? Look at the cover of this book and every other book I have written. Way up in the top, where you can't miss it, are the words, "Learn How to Win!!!" This is not an idle statement. Most people do not know how to win.

The psyche of the casinos has a lot to do with it. They have this beautiful atmosphere, soft lights, pleasant music, gorgeous cocktail waitresses, hiding places for drifting husbands, and, above all, the possibility of minor fortunes for the good players.

Many people get caught up in this psyche—more than you might think. Let's face it, the casinos have the carrots to hold out in front of the rabbits, and they utilize every opportunity, especially, taking advantage of the weaknesses of the average, weekly bettor. This hype is just too much for him. He starts making bets, much higher than is called for, in an effort to play 'up' to the high rollers at the table.

This poor dope drops two dimes in the Sunday collection basket and acts like Godfrey Goldbricks in a casino. He thinks this is the way to act. In all actuality, he is caught up in the elaborate settings and loses all control.

On the way to the casino he is clutching his last $200 of gambling money and praying that he can at least break even. As soon as the cocktail waitress gives him his first free brandy, he starts losing his cool. You know when reality hits him? On the way home in the car when he gets to the toll plaza and finds out his last $2 went to the friendly dealer who gave him the time of day after that dealer beat him eleven straight hands on the blackjack table.

Wise up! Try and use some common sense when gambling. Is there anything logical (Little Three), about risking money on games that you have only a fragment of knowledge about? Of course not! Incidentally, did you notice how the three items I listed in the 'Little Three' awareness chapter came into play? Logic, theory, and trends will pop up over and over.

You must set limits on your losses. Otherwise, the aura of the surroundings will dull your senses and dictate moves you would not normally make.

By bringing down a $300 bankroll and limiting your losses to 50% or $150, this allows you to play smart and easy. If you were playing with only $150 and lost a few hands, the 'scared money' syndrome would engulf you and you'd allow your bankroll to determine your moves rather than the best percentage plays. You would begin making bets that provide larger pay-offs, figuring that if you won you'd have the money to continue playing. If you don't think you have the discipline to set a loss limit and quit when you reach it, then you'd better stop gambling right this minute and take up a safer pastime like mountain climbing or bull fighting. You'd have a better chance.

Remember, you do not have to stick to the percentage of loss limits that I laid out for you. In roulette, you could lose 40%, 35%, 30%, or whatever amount you set. But set a limit; an absolute, final cut-off point where you will no longer delve into your pocket for betting money.

If you set this loss limit, you will never go broke. Never!!!! It's a virtual guarantee. Suppose your loss limit is 50% of $600, and you lose it on this particular day. You bring home $300, but you have money to return to battle. The next time you go to a casino, you bring the $300 and again set your loss limit at 50%. If you again find the trends going against you and you lose your limit, it is only $150. This time you bring home $150. But again, you are not broke. Your next trip will start with $150. The most you can drop is $75. The main thing is that you still have money to return to battle.

It's impossible to go broke. Impossible because you can never lose more than 50% of your stake at any time. You know something? I talk to thousands of people who gamble, and each one of them needs that starting bankroll to play. If they don't have it, they can't compete.

Oh, you're not going to like this restrictive method of playing, but you must admit it is a powerful tool. You are playing an even game. Stop thinking that you can win every time. You can't, and you won't. But, you can play intelligently. Setting loss limits is a tremendously important factor in making you learn how to win.

# BANKROLL                    4

## Win Goals

Just because you've set a loss limit doesn't mean there isn't another side of the coin. This is the important part. This is the part that takes guts, nerve, cockiness, and discipline. It is learning how to win. In other words, it is a win goal.

Ever set a win goal when you're betting? You haven't? Well, then how the devil do you know when it's time to leave? I know, you set time limits such as playing for one hour, three hours, or some such period.

I hear people say, "I'm going to play for an hour and then quit, whether I'm ahead or behind". Well, I'll tell you something. Anytime I listen to somebody talk like that I know right away they *are* a behind. But, that's another story.

Let's go back to the time punchers. Never play by the clock. What happens if after you reach the end of youe predetermined time play you are ahead $320? Do you just get up and leave? Here you're on a winning trend, you've got the house against the wall, and you decide to up and leave. Do you know how hard it is to get on a winning streak? It's plenty hard. When you finally do get things going your way, why get up and leave? There is no logical explanation for a silly move like that.

At the same time, you can't expect trends to last forever. They don't. While they are producing good results, you have to know how to handle them. The chapters on money management will show you how.

For now, I just want you to be aware of the need for win goals. You remember in the previous chapter how I talked about loss limits? That was a hard, fast, final, cut and dried finish to your betting. You always have this loss limit to restrict the amount of your losses.

But you do not set win limits. Wouldn't that be a dumb move? How can you set a limit on how much you will win? No—you set win goals; not limits. First of all, you have to reach your win goal and then go for the moon. You notice I didn't say win limit. You must set a win goal—a figure in mind that you set as your goal for that day.

Since I am a conservative person, I set conservative goals. My goal is 20%. That means I want to win 20% of the amount that I take to the casino. In case you don't realize it, that is quite a feat even though it doesn't sound very high.

In reality I am only seeking a 10% return, and that, too, is a healthy chunk. I set my goal a little higher so as to guarantee a win for the day and still have an excess amount in which to shoot for a bigger return.

Let's put that in layman's terms. Suppose I take $1000 to the casino. My decisions are all based on that $1000. If I were to play roulette, for instance, my loss limit would be 50% or $500. I may quit when I reach a $400 loss, but I sure as heck won't lose a dime more than $500.

On the plus side, I really want a 10% return; $100 profit. If I do get ahead, I don't want to leave that table in the middle of a hot trend. That's why I set my win goal at 20% or $200. When I reach it, I break it in half and put $100 in my pocket, which is really 10% of my starting bankroll. I still have $100 in excess money to use in going for higher profits. Even if I lose that $100 excess, I already have pocketed $100 as guaranteed winnings for that day.

This entire system is detailed in the money management chapters. You must set win goals in advance. Maybe you want to set a higher percentage as your goal. Maybe you'll set a lower amount. That's your own personal preference. That's your own personal theory as to what you believe you can make.

Some girls like fat guys. Others like skinny guys. Some like 'em tall. Others want the cute little tiny guys. They all have their own goals that they want to go for. Who's to say any of them are wrong? But, at least they do set the goals.

The same is true in gambling. Set your win goal and set it low enough so that it's easy to reach. You'll get in the habit of winning and you will love it.

Take my word for it.

# 5   BANKROLL

## Play Or Win

This chapter ought to really hit home to many readers. The reason why many people who go to a casino lose is that they don't play to win. They don't know how! Sound silly? It isn't.

Think of it for a minute. How many times have you heard somebody say something like this, "Oh, I'd like to win, but since I'm only going once this month, I just want to play". Or, "I was up $250. But, it was early and we were going to stay over for the shows so there was nothing else to do but play".

How about this beauty? "I was in the casino about 1½ hours, and was ahead $325. The bus wasn't leaving for several hours, so I decided to go for the kill. I lost back the $325 and about $100 of my own, but I had fun."

Can you believe these jerks? "I had fun!" Who the hell has fun losing money, especially after they were ahead a sizable amount? You wanna know something? I really think these people believe they did have fun. They don't know why it hurts so much when they get home, as they're too far out of it to understand how foolish they were.

Maybe you're one of the people who believes that the fun in a casino is derived from 'playing' and not 'winning'. Well, I've got another scoop for you. It's a beautiful, satisfying feeling when you walk out of the casino a winner.

I know you're going to say that you want to win, but you don't know how. You get ahead a couple of dollars, and it fails to enter your brain that maybe you should be looking to run with the profits.

So many people go to the casinos to play, to kill the day and to be part of the excitement. They say they want to win, but they get ahead and what do they do? Why, sit at the table and continue to play. Sure, it's fun. But, where do you differentiate between your main purpose and your individual pleasures?

The professional gambler does not play according to a watch. His purpose upon entering the casino is to get ahead a certain amount of money based on his starting bankroll, manage it, and play until his trends begin to decline. I am not trying to make you a professional gambler. I am only trying to make you aware of the proper way to approach the tables.

The casinos present a tremendous, enticing package to all comers. They give you a fair chance to beat them. They offer you the chance to compete at various games. Take your pick. There's no rule that says you have to play a certain game. You can quit any time you want or play as long as the doors are open.

Think about it. Do you gamble just to play, or to be involved? Or, do you gamble to win? It's a big point. If you are the type of person who goes to the casinos just to be a part of the action, you're not going to gain a thing out of this book. In the long run, you'll be whacked.

But if you play to win, I mean really concentrate on all the aspects of the game you're involved in, then eventually you will be a consistent winner. I didn't say big winner. I said consistent winner. There's a difference.

Think it over for a minute. Really dwell on your own situation. Do you play to play, or do you play to win? Again — there's a difference.

# BANKROLL 6

## Basic Table Minimums

I would just like to spend a few moments on this subject. Table minimum means the lowest amount that you can wager at a particular game. In Atlantic City, most tables have minimums of $5. They are usually indicated by a red card on the table. This means that the lowest bet at that table is $5. If a white card is shown, the minimum is $3. Yellow signifies $10. Green is $25. Black is $100 minimum.

There are also maximums shown on these cards. That is to prohibit high rollers from using a double up or Martingale progression method of betting whereby the player keeps doubling his bet, waiting for the hit that will return everything he laid out plus at least one unit of profit.

These maximums help the casinos restrict the wagering; but, more importantly, they act as a control or loss limit for the house. Isn't it funny that the casinos with all their money still set these loss limits. They must be an important part of gambling. Yet, the novice has to be hit over the head, and dragged out of the casino by his feet, to get him to leave before he bets all his money, his wife, his kids, etc.

When the casinos are crowded, the table minimums are pushed up to higher amounts which forces the players with short bankrolls to risk more of their money on individual hands or rolls of the dice.

These minimum rules destroy more gamblers than you can imagine. In Las Vegas, you can find $2 minimum tables, $1 tables, and even $.50 games. That keeps you in the hunt. You have a chance to 'stay alive' until your streak comes.

My only beef with Atlantic City casinos is that the $5 tables are too high for many people. A guy sauntering into the blackjack section has $100 in his kick, and big dreams in his head. Where's he going with a $5 table? Maybe he loses the first four hands, one of which called for an extra bet on a double down hand, and already he is down 25% of his stake.

You think he ain't scared? Man, he's saying the rosary to himself in between cursing out his bad fortune. If it was a $1 or $2 table, he'd be in a comfortable situation.

How about the poor guy who brings his chick to the casino for a night out? He's planned a nice dinner, a show, and a few hours at the tables to impress his new girl. After the dinner show, he has about $70 left to show her some action. He nearly faints when he sees all the table minimums are $10. He figured they'd both play for two or three hours at a $3 table. There's no way he can get into these games, at least he shouldn't, not with that short bankroll. The table minimums did him in.

You should have at least 30 times the amount of the minimums of the table you play at. I know it's hard for many people due to these higher minimums, but that's the way it is.

You don't have the proper starting amount? Then don't play. You can't expect to be competitive with scared money. And that's exactly what your money becomes, when you are in over your head.

Don't be ashamed to play at the tables that give you the lowest possible minimum standard, maybe even $2. Jump right in. You'll be able to play comfortably and at ease. If it embarrasses you that one of your cronies might see you playing at a $2 table, then you've got some problems. Forget your silly ego, and learn how to win.

# 7　BANKROLL

## Summary On Bankroll

Ok, let's wrap up this part of the Big Four with a warning that if you don't understand how important the bankroll is, you're making a gigantic mistake. Since it is the starting block for anything you gamble on, it is important that you play within the confines of that amount.

You need go no further than your own personal experiences in gambling. Don't you feel more comfortable when you have a decent amount of money with you rather than squeezing your gambling money out of more important functions?

So many, many times I give lectures at senior citizen centers, and this subject comes up. Most of these people look forward to a day at the casinos, really go there with high expectations. In the back of their minds they're telling themselves that they'll probably lose, but way, way up in the corner of their brains, hope springs eternal. They're looking for that hit. They're looking for the sweet smile of Lady Luck to shine on them. Well, Lady Luck is a fantasy. She isn't allowed to go into casinos, race tracks, or bookie joints. Luck does not enter into gambling. Only the Big Four — that's all you can expect to bring with you.

1. Bankroll
2. Knowledge of the Game
3. Money Management
4. Discipline

If you're missing any one of them, you're in deep trouble.

I'll give you an idea of how the casinos view the senior citizen groups that converge on their parlors daily, especially in Atlantic City. First of all, the people are taken down and back in a beautiful luxury bus complete with comfortable chairs, air conditioning, and sometimes refreshments.

The price is only about $15. But wait, when you get to Atlantic City a hostess will get on the buss and give you a coupon that will allow you to redeem $10 in quarters; and, in many cases, the casino will give a credit towards a nice meal in one of their fine restaurants.

That means, for all intents and purposes, the trip is free. Yes, it is. Do you think that the casinos are unaware that the senior citizens bring only short bankrolls? Of course they're not. They are fully aware that these people descend upon the tables & slots with short or scared money. (In most cases, both.)

The casinos have each senior citizen programmed at $30 per head. That means they are willing to bring these people down free and settle for $30. We know that is not a lot of money, but multiply it by the 40 or 45 people on a bus and you have about $1300 a pop. Add in the $10 in quarters that most people put back into the games, and you can see only the casinos make money. With all their extravagance, they settle for $30 per person.

And how about the people who come down in the buses with their $40 & $100 bankrolls? Do they set realistic win figures? Of course not. They want the left wing of the casino.

I ask these people what their starting bankroll is. The answers range from $25 to $100. I am not knocking these people for their small bankrolls. I am only trying to make them aware that it is not enough. Not when they are forced to play at tables that provide $5 betting minimums.

So, most people rush to the slot machines where they only have to put in 25¢ at a time in the hopes that they can stay 'alive' longer. That puts them right into the meat grinder, as they are now playing a game where the vig, or drain, is about 13% against them.

This is all because they don't have the starting bankroll. The casinos in Las Vegas have the small minimum tables and you can compete with a $50 cache. In Atlantic City, you must wait until your bankroll meets the qualifications that I laid out.

You need a bankroll, my friend, or you can't compete — or shouldn't compete. Think about it.

# KNOWLEDGE OF THE GAME — SLOTS

## 1

## Knowledge, What Is It?

We move into the second phase of the Big Four; Knowledge of the Game. What is knowledge? As the dictionary states: "cognition, learning, science, skill from practice". You need this skill at whatever game you hope to bet on. If it is poker, you sure better know the difference between a flush and a straight. In blackjack, every percentage move must be automatic.

When I insist that you have a knowledge of the game you will compete at, I don't just mean knowledge *of,* I mean perfect *at.* If you are good, it is not enough. If you are very good, you will still be lacking. If you are perfect, you have about a 50-50 chance of winning.

Can you absorb that? A perfect player still has only a 50-50 chance of winning. And people who are way less than good still try to win at gambling. What gall!

How can you have the audacity to risk your money at games in which you are not perfect? In this book I am covering slots and roulette. These are games in which knowledge does not come into much play— only money management, and discipline. But it is imperative that you have a complete idea of each of the games, so as to be aware of what your chances of winning are.

In betting on blackjack, horses, sports, or cards, complete knowledge is important, along with money management & discipline. However, the games in this book are best described as 'games of chance'. Your approach to them should be guarded, and in all cases you must be wary of the pitfalls that you face; otherwise, how can you avoid them?

I shall cover each of the games, showing background, vigorish against you, and method of play, based on money management and discipline, in the event you insist on playing these particular games.

I take my gambling seriously, and I hope you do, too. If you don't, it's only a matter of time before you get whacked. Agreed, a lot of people gamble every day, but many believe they're going to lose anyway, so don't take the time to learn everything they can about the subject.

I'll tell you why people won't go to the trouble of perfecting the game they play. They're too lazy. Out and out too stupid to take the time to find out what the heck is going on. The excuse is always the same: "Well, I only go to the casinos once every two weeks. It's not worth it for me to go to all that trouble".

Can you believe that? Can you believe a relatively intelligent person making a statement like that? They bring hard earned money to a table, get whacked, and shrug it off because they only go to a casino twice a month—for fun. This is not an isolated example. I hear this type nonsense all the time, and I still can't buy it.

Ever hear of a person who doesn't know how to

ski entering the giant slalom? Or a guy that's been driving for three weeks entering the Indy 500? How many people apply for secretarial jobs who can't type or take shorthand? Not many, I would assume, because your chances of getting the job would be about zero. Well then why try to gamble, if you don't know how. That's why I have included knowledge of the game in the Big Four. It is imperative that you know the game.

What is knowledge? It is 25% of the Big Four. I don't give a rat's tail if you have $20,000 to gamble with. If you don't understand the game you're playing, eventually this lack of knowledge will get to that bankroll.

Don't be good; be perfect. Know everything there is to know about the game you will tackle. Why not? It'll help you to win, and isn't that why you're reading this book in the first place?

# 2 KNOWLEDGE OF THE GAME — SLOTS

## Slots

What can I tell you? What key do I have for opening up that pesty machine and sending those thousands of silver dollars flowing into your pockets? There is no answer. There is no way to come up with a system to beat these bandits. And that's just what they are, bandits.

They sit there, all bright and shiny, with their left arm pointed to heaven, of all places, pleading with you to fill their stomachs with your silver dollars, quarters, anything. It is sooooo easy. So exciting. Place a coin into the slot, pull the handle, and pray in anticipation that this time those symbols will light up the jackpot. You missed. Well, maybe next time. Dreamer!!

I will give you some background information on the slots, some figures on vigorish, and some discipline factors. The rest is up to you. You want to play; go ahead, it's your money.

Slot machines reared their pretty heads in 1895 when Charles Fey, an enterprising young mechanic, invented the first machine. It was named the Liberty Bell. Fey not only invented it, but distributed his prizes to gambling houses who split the take on a 50-50 basis.

Fey did not use the fruits that are seen on today's machines. His invention carried card symbols, such as diamonds, hearts, spades, etc. These devices were instant successes, and naturally lured other enterprising "inventors". Herbert Mills, an arcade games manufacturer, improved on Fey's invention and the battle was on.

The first machines had three reels, but used only ten symbols on each reel, as opposed to today's bandits which contain twenty symbols per reel.

If you were to take off the back of a slot machine, besides the usual amount of wires, levers, and screws, you would see three reels which are activated when a coin is deposited and the arm is pulled down. These three reels spin for pre-determined seconds, and then come to a stop in 1-2-3- order, showing three of the symbols in the window on the front of the machine.

Since each reel contains 20 symbols, such as cherries, plums, bars, oranges, etc., let's find the possibility of one certain combination showing up. Merely multiply the symbols on each reel, such as $20 \times 20 \times 20$ which equals 8,000 possible combinations. If one particular machine had it's jackpot based on three bars and there was only one bar on each reel, the chances of that combination showing up would be 7,999 to 1. That's because there are 7,999 ways to lose, as opposed to one way of winning.

Naturally, to find the correct chances of your hitting a jackpot, you would have to examine each reel to find out how many bars are on these reels, and then figure your percentage chances.

For instance the first reel might have seven bars, the second five bars, and the third reel, one bar. You would work out your possible chances of having those bars all meet together and arrive at the percentage possibility of a jackpot. Multiply $7 \times 5$ equals 35, $\times 1$ for a total of only 35 ways that the jackpot on that machine can be reached out of 8000 possible total combinations. Would you call that a fruitless (excuse the pun) endeavor? Well, if it isn't fruitless, it sure is rough.

Of course, in the meantime, there are smaller pay-offs, such as one cherry, two cherries, three oranges, three plums, etc. The pay-offs are not jackpots, as the pay-off is smaller returns, such as 3 coins, 14 coins, etc.

Understand this about the slot machines. They are programmed to return a certain amount of money based on their input. That amount might by 87%. That means, for every $100 that is poured into a machine, it is programmed to return $87. The $13 that it retains is the vig you are fighting.

The machines are set to return a certain number of coins when a combination shows. By multiplying all of the possible combinations and applying the number of coins that it will kick off, you will find out what that certain percentage is. Take a normal $1 silver dollar machine. If the vig is set for 7%, that means the house retains 93% for that particular slot. All of the pay-off combinations, which might total 45 for example, have different pay-offs, such as 500 coins, 250 coins, 50 coins, 18 coins; all the way down to 2 coins for one cherry. If you could tabulate all of the returns and apply it to the total intake, you get your percentage of vig. That doesn't mean, naturally, that if you put $1 into the slot, you get immediately a return of .87 on a slot that has a 13% vig. The percentages are spread over thousands of plays, and not in any set pattern.

If the machine is set to return 6800 coins out of all of their combinations as against a possible 8000 inserted, that merely means that the house is keeping 15% of the 8000 coins, or 1200, and giving back 6800, or 85%. The state decides on what that percentage will be, and the casinos must stay within those laws. Maybe one machine retains only 8%, and the one next to it retains 11%. In the overall slot section, the house does stay within the letter of the law.

In Las Vegas there are some machines that return 96% and 97% of their intake. The operator can still realize a handsome profit from these machines, and at the same time provide excellent advertising about his establishment. There is absolutely nothing that beats the hot word that a certain game can be beaten.

Since the days of Charlie Fey, the bandits have improved to the point that they offer various combinations of symbols, such as bars, triple bars, 7's, bells, and all types of figures to lure the superstitious player.

But the percentages remain the same, and the house always retains the edge. It's called the hammer, and it hits you over the head every time you pull that arm down. Isn't it funny...you probably don't even feel it.

# 3 KNOWLEDGE OF THE GAME — SLOTS

## Percentages In Slots

Let's get a little technical for awhile. To better illustrate what you are fighting at the machines, let's try and give you an idea as to how to figure the vigorish against you.

Suppose we wanted to find out exactly what our chances of winning were. That could only be done by examining each reel and counting every symbol that is shown. Since this can never happen, as the casinos do not have the time to allow each player to satisfy their whims, we can only guess as to the number of symbols of one kind may be found on a single reel. For example, breakdowns may be as follows:

| REEL 1 | REEL 2 | REEL 3 |
|--------|--------|--------|
| Plums 5 | Plums 4 | Plums 4 |
| Cherries 3 | Cherries 6 | Anything |
| Oranges 4 | Oranges 6 | Oranges 4 |

**CHERRIES:** A payoff on the cherries would be figured by multiplying the three on the first reel, by the six on the second, and any one of the twenty symbols on the third reel. This gives you 360 combinations. That means of the 8000 combos, 360 could be this payoff, and, of course, the return is only about four coins. Go over every possible pay-out that is shown on the front end of the machine, and figure how many ways each could be made and the number of coins that are returned, such as 14 coins for 3 oranges, 18 coins for three plums, and so on. If you put 8000 straight coins into a certain slot machine and know exactly what each payoff for all the programmed wins would produce, you would see what your percentage of winning would be. You can be sure that the machine is not set to return more than 8000 coins over a certain number of cycles.

Back to our explanation on the cherries. When the single cherry appears on the first reel, simply multiply the number of cherries on reel 1, times the fourteen times that the cherry does not appear on reel 2, times anything that will appear twenty times on reel three, and you have $3 \times 14 \times 20$, or 840 combinations. If the pay-off is 2 coins, that slot kicks out 1,680 total coins for that situation.

If it were plums, the table would read $5 \times 4 \times 4$, or 80 possible combinations. If the three plums were programmed to return 10 coins, there would be 800 coins in all returned when three plums appeared.

As I stated in the previous chapter, the 8000 possible combinations may be broken down to return 6,800 coins based on these various possibilities. The house still retains a 15% profit margin or vig.

These machines are not 'fixed' to eat up thousands of coins before the pay-offs start occurring. But they are programmed to return only a percentage of the total number of combinations. For instance, one machine could conceivably kick off two jack-pots in 20 pulls of the arm, and also return a sizable chunk of money on the lesser combinations, all in the space of twenty or thirty pulls. But who is to say when this will occur. That's why they call it gambling.

I'm not trying to confuse you with a bunch of mathematical mumbo-jumbo, just attempting to make you aware of what the slots are about. I hear so many people at the slots pouring in coins and moaning that the casinos have the machines fixed. Baloney. They're not fixed, and the casinos don't have to cheat. They are working on percentages, and it is those percentages, plus your lack of bankroll, plus your lack of knowledge, plus your lack of money management, plus your lack of D-I-S-C-I-P-L-I-N-E that destroys you.

A final note on this chapter. Go get yourself 8000 quarters to equal the number of possible combinations that could occur. Simply place a coin in the slot for 8000 consecutive pulls. Each time there is a pay-off, you put the winnings in your pocket, and continue to insert one of the starting 8000 coins into the bandit.

When you are finished with the 8000 starting coins, take out all of the pay-offs that you stuck in your pocket. The amount of these pay-offs, as applied to the starting bankroll, will give you the percentage that the machine is returning. This is not a fool-proof system, as you could have repeat combinations occur both for and against the player, since the machine is set to show random combinations.

This will give you an idea of the vig you are facing, but nobody will go to all of this trouble, as most people want to try other slots.

Look over these examples until you completely understand the functions of the one-armed bandit. It is not complicated, and like I've said all along, the logic of it stands out — or is it illogic???

# 4 KNOWLEDGE OF THE GAME — SLOTS

## System Players

You think there aren't system players in slots? You've gotta be kidding. Since most gamblers are superstitious, you can be sure that the slot players are right up there with their zany ideas. Following are some theories that players have come up and asked me about. Maybe you've tried some of these yourself:

a) Always play the machines on the end, because they are programmed to return more money so as to prime the other players to get involved.

b) Stand and watch the person play a certain machine for a period of time, and then when he leaves that machine step up and play it because it's due to be hit.

c) Only play the machines that have the bars.

d) Never play the machines that have the bars.

e) Only play the machines that have the 7's.

f) Never play the machines that have the 7's.

g) Play the rhythm system, which is a certain method of pulling the handle in a pre-determined time span to take advantage of the mechanism not being able to reset itself before it is forced to operate again.

h) Play only at night, because the casinos set higher returns after 6 PM.

i) Play only at machines at certain sides of a casino.

Put all of this nonsense behind you. Most of these so called "systems" can be thrown out by an illogical approach to an already firm percentage setup. In simple terms, the slot machine will return anywhere from 85% to 97%, and all the planning in the world isn't going to change those percentages.

Look at how ridiculous some of these assumptions are:

a) I've been listening to this poppycock about the big paying machines put on the end where players can readily get to them. Do you know how many 'end' machines there are in just one casino? Go into a casino and look at how many are in prominent positions. You'd never be able to find even ten that would classify as end machines. Go ahead, try and find ten that stand out more than the others. You can't. There are at least 70 machines that could be designated to be in prominent places. This idea is a myth.

b) By standing and watching somebody play a machine for a period of time only keeps you away from pouring your money into another machine. This idea is another fabrication of the novice's belief that when an occurance doesn't happen, for instance, a hit on a slot machine, than the opposite is 'due' to occur. This thinking has destroyed more gamblers than any other mode of illogical misinterpretation.

c,d,e,f) The machines do not pay off higher

amounts based on the type of symbol that is used, such as bars, bells, 7's, etc. They are merely pawns to indicate a winning or losing combination. Don't judge your play on this factor.

     g) The rhythm system had some valid arguments in its favor years ago in the mid-forties when defects in the slot machines were detected and exploited by enterprising 'mechanics'. The manufacturers soon found and corrected the loopholes in their machines. This system faded away, but the stories continued. Let's assume there was a rhythm system. Do you think you could find it before the operators? Come on, be honest. Do you think these casino operators are asleep?

     h) Play only at night? How could the casinos possibly adjust 500 machines to change pay-off's? First, it would be foolhardy. Second, impossible. Third, I guess the Casino Control Commission would have a field day with that particular casino who pulled this stuff.

     i) Why would the 'house' put hot machines on one side of the casino and cold machines on the other? How could they know which side the majority of players would flock to.

     Get something straight about all of these crazy notions about what the casinos do to get the slot player. They don't have to do a thing. They have the 4% to 13% working for them, and people standing in line to take a shot. All of these crazy myths become invented out of isolated cases, and as they are handed down through the years, they pick up steam, and become more absurd.

Do you ever read the billboards entering Atlantic City as you drive through Absecon, the town on the outskirts? What is plastered all over most of these ads? You named it — slots. They boldly pronounce that such and such a casino has:

a) The best slots

b) The highest paying slots

c) The most money paid over a certain period at the slots

d) The most jackpots in the past six months at the slots

e) The biggest single pay-off in town on the slots

Well, if the people were banging so much money at these machines, why would the casinos keep telling you to come in and take another shot at them. Are they saying they like to get whacked at the slot machines? Of course not. These ads are all probably true, but it doesn't show you the comparison intake based on how much money was wagered.

Ah, the power of suggestion.

Just realize one simple single thing about the slots, and you can put the whole exercise into perspective. When you walk into a casino and go up to a slot machine, you are fighting a vigorish of anywhere from 4% to 13%.

# 5 KNOWLEDGE OF THE GAME — SLOTS

## Should I Play The Slots?

If you have read all of the figures outlined for you in the previous chapters and still want to play the slots, go ahead. But first go back a few chapters to what I said about people who gamble, and how they are basically put into two separate categories: those who bet to win and those who bet just to bet. In the latter group are most people, because they enjoy playing so much that they never learned how to win — and quit a winner.

Slot players are primarily in this second group. A lot of them realize how tough it is to win, and yet they still play because they love the thrill of competing so much. People tell me every day how thrilling it is to play the slots. Many of them out and out believe that they're going to lose anyway, so why not play something they enjoy. Man, what crazy thinking.

But getting back to the basic question. Should you play the slots? Well, billions of coins are dropped into slot machines every year, so people are going to continue to play, regardless of what anyone says. The lure is just too great.

So play, but let's look at the intelligent way to approach it. Money management. . . This applies to the one-armed bandits, just like any other game of chance.

Set aside an amount of money that you would like to wager on the slots. Since you're going to play anyway, you may as well play with some type of control. I'm going to give you a very, very strong disciplined method of getting in a little time at the slots, as long as you realize that the bulk of your starting bankroll should be used to play the games that offer you the least chance of losing. Maybe after using this method and getting in a fair amount of times on the machines, you will concentrate on the other games, learn how to win at them, and eventually shun the bandits altogether.

Let's assume you bring $300 to the casino. Set aside a percentage of that $300 which will constitute a separate bankroll for the slots. For instance, you decide that of your starting bankroll, 25% will be invested into the one-armed bandits. That should quiet your craving for action on these machines for that day. This means $75 will be wagered on slots, and the other $225 held for the other games of your choice.

Since you don't want to get wiped out on the first machine, you should separate your slots stake into sessions. The amount of the sessions will all be equal in value, and played at a machine until a predetermined loss limit is reached or a predetermined win goal is hit.

If $75 is your stake, break it down into sessions, depending on your own individual level of comfortable play. We'll start at the 25¢ slots. You decide to invest $5 in a machine, so the bankroll is divided into 15 sessions @ $5 per session. That gives you fifteen machines at $5 per session. The next chapter goes over the money management for the sessions, so right now I am concentrating on your bankroll control. For a $75 stake at the slots, your sessions could be as follows:

**SLOT BANKROLL — $75** (which is 25% of $300 total bankroll) — Select one of these:
| | | |
|---|---|---|
| a) 10 Sessions | @ | $7.50 per session |
| b) 15 Sessions | @ | $5.00 per session |
| c) 20 Sessions | @ | $3.75 per session |
| d) 25 Sessions | @ | $3.00 per session |
| e) 50 Sessions | @ | $1.50 per session |

**SLOT BANKROLL — $50** (which is 20% of $250 overall bankroll) — Select one of these:
| | | |
|---|---|---|
| a) 10 Sessions | @ | $5.00 per session |
| b) 20 Sessions | @ | $2.50 per session |
| c) 25 Sessions | @ | $2.00 per session |
| d) 50 Sessions | @ | $1.00 per session |

**SLOT BANKROLL — $20** (which is 25% of $80 bankroll) — Select one of these:
| | | |
|---|---|---|
| a) 8 Sessions | @ | $2.50 per session |
| b) 10 Sessions | @ | $2.00 per session |
| c) 16 Sessions | @ | $1.25 per session |
| d) 20 Sessions | @ | $1.00 per session |

You laugh? You laugh at money management in slots? You ought to laugh at the idea of even playing slots. I do not encourage you to attack these monsters, but only advise a plan of attack if you do 'have' to play them. You would be astonished at the amount of people who just 'have' to take a shot at them. Much like other things we do in life, that defy reason or logic.

Mr. Paine N. Gutt has a very weak stomach and has been told by nine doctors that he can eat anything in the world except a pizza pie, with hot sauce and peppers. You know what Mr. Gutt craves? You guessed it, he just 'has' to have that pizza. He just has to try it, knowing all too well he'll end up with another stomach ache. To make matters worse, he has to order it with extra sauce and a double order of peppers.

You think he will listen to reason? Do you think a million slot players are going to walk past the slot machines? No—on both counts. So, I set up a means of attack. You know all about the Big Four. Well, the breakdown I've given you, and the amount of the sessions is made to coincide with your bankroll. Since you don't need any knowledge to play slots, we slide over to money management & discipline, and that is covered in the next chapter.

Go back over the session breakdown and study the patterns. Then set up your bankroll for the next trip to the casinos. Arrive at your own percentage for play at the one-armed bandits. It could be 10%, 20% or 25%, or whatever makes you feel comfortable. Break it down into sessions. Again, whatever makes you feel comfortable, regardless of how many you want. It could be five sessions or machines, or it could be 30 sessions or machines. You be the judge (much like a guy on trial, and he ends up as his own judge, jury, and executioner—but that's another story).

Should I play slots? No. . .but if you must — use the Big Four. A final thought on anybody who just has to play these machines. I agree heartily that they are a lot of fun, and I've pulled a few muscles myself, trying to get them to pour out their hearts to me. Oh, I've won my share of jackpots, but nowhere near enough to compensate for the amount that I've fed them. You are going to have to make a big, big, big decision. Do I want to play, or do I want to win? This method that I am giving you will in no way make you win, nor is it a super secret system that will unlock those machines.

It is a method of control that will undoubtedly help you manage your money and reduce your losses. This loss limit will make for a tremendous savings for you over a period of time. Read it again, and see if you can grasp the theory of this method. All of these tiny pieces will one day fall into line for you, and you will see the light go on. Until that happens, you're just another disbeliever.

# KNOWLEDGE OF THE GAME — SLOTS  **6**

## Slots, Money Management & Discipline

Okay, you've taken a percentage of your total bankroll and set it aside for slots play. Let's use the $300 total bankroll with a 25% slice or $75 slot stake.

You decide to divide it into 15 sessions at $5 per session. That means you can play at 15 different slot machines, but only 15. You can play at less, based on whether you win the pre-determined amount of your win goal prior to hitting 15 machines. But you cannot play at any more than the 15, as this ties in with your Loss Limit of $75 for your slot play. Don't deviate from this restriction. If 15 sessions @ $5 equals the amount you set aside for slot play, don't exceed it — period. The same system prevails as to setting win goals and loss limits. In other words, discipline is still the bottom line. Before you go into the slot section with your $75, you set your loss limit and win goal. Set the loss limit at 60%. That means at each $5 session, you can lose absolutely no more than $3 and not one quarter more.

When you lose the pre-determined $3, or any amount up to it, that session is over, and you move on the next session. Naturally, if you are at a machine that is 'dry' and not paying off anything, you don't have to stand there and pour in your full 60%. Let us suppose that you play 25¢ a pop and lose nine straight decisions. It's fairly obvious that the trend on this machine is against you. You don't have to get slapped in the face seven times by your girl friend to get the idea that she is in a bad mood. With your wife it's probably a different story, and you have to take it.

But with the slots, as in all gambling, you don't have to take it. Walk away. Even if you've only lost $2.25 of the pre-determined $3, that session is over. Put the extra $2.75 in your pocket, never to be touched again that day.

Again you ask, "If I'm going to lose $3 per machine, why not just bring $3 to the machine with me?" Again, I tell you — discipline. Learn to win. Learn how to acquire discipline. Learn how NOT to bet down to your last quarter.

You don't want to set 60% as your loss limit? Get your own figure and stick to it. Maybe you'll set it at 40%, 50%, or maybe even 25%; but not higher than 60%. Then you're pushing. Okay, you've set your loss limits; now go for your win goals. This will be very difficult for anyone to do, because you will find it hard to take the small wins that have to be based against the small bankroll. I will give you two methods of setting win goals, and you decide which one you find easier to accept.

A) **STRAIGHT 60%.** This is based on the fact that you set 60% of the $5 session money as your loss limit, so you turn around and set 60% of the $5 as your win goal. In other words, you will play until you win a total of $3 which guarantees a win for that machine. After you win the 60% ($3) at this machine, you set 50% of the $3 aside which is $1.50. This assures you of leaving that machine a winner which is what gambling is all about.

But, since I adhere to the theory that trends dominate in gambling, I don't want to pull you away from the machine that just kicked $3 in coin out to you. Therefore, you have $1.50 excess to play with at that same slot machine. Don't go giving me that nonsense that since you won $3, the machine is 'due' to go dry. There's that silly word "due", again.

With this $1.50 excess you put the quarters back in. Everytime you win two coins, take one quarter out and place it with your original $1.50 guarantee. The other quarter stays with the excess. If you hit a four-teen quarter pay-off, 50% goes with the guarantee and 50% stays with the excess. You continue at that machine for as long as the excess lasts. When it is gone —so are you. But if you hit a couple of pay-offs with the excess, at least you increased the original $1.50 by 50% of each of those hits. There's no telling when you can catch a hot machine and continue to win, all the time being protected by your loss limits which are set before you play. Protect both your original starting session money and your excess money after a guar-anteed win.

This system, called straight 60, calls for the im-mediate acceleration to a certain percentage before taking any profit. But the important part is in setting the percentage before you begin, so that your goal is always on your mind and provides you direction.

Incidentally, I'm well aware that these examples of winning $1.50 per machine are way below the standards you have set for yourself. You want the key to the casino vault with a tiny starting bankroll that wouldn't pay the daily electric bill in the baccarat room of the smallest casino in Las Vegas. Swallow your silly dreams and get in touch with reality. You can shoot for the moon when you bring the proper bankroll to war. Until then, read on.

B) **THE CHICKEN APPROACH.** The second method is more for the faint of heart and is a rather conservative system. The name of it is aptly called "The Chicken Approach". It is for those people who love to gamble, but are absolutely petrified of losing. I don't mean they're worried about dropping a few dollars. I mean they are petrified. They lose $25 in a casino and spend the ride home condemning everyone even remotely connected with their trip to the tables.

They really love the action, and breaking even is written up in their personal diary as akin to World War III. So the trick is to afford them the chance to pick up small, but consistent, pay-offs.

The preliminary work is exactly the same as in the straight 60 method. You set aside a percentage of your original bankroll, and, in this case, we continue to work with the $75 slot bankroll which is 25% of your original amount of $300. Again, it is broken into sessions, and again you decide on 15 sessions @ $5 each. For you $1 slot players, you're going to have to adjust your sessions to coincide with your bankroll. If it allows you to play $1 slots, good, go to it. If it doesn't, then accept your deficient money supply and play at the 25¢ slots which is in line with your pocketbook and not your dreams.

The difference in this method is in the goals. The straight method called for a pre-determined amount before you took your guarantee. The "Chicken Approach" calls for immediate rat-holing, or pocketing of a pay-off.

The Loss Limit must be set, just like in all games, and is up to the discretion of each individual. Let's place 30% on the session. When you lose anywhere up to 30% ($1.50) of your session money of $5, the session is over.

But, the win goal is immediately put into effect. Let's say you place a quarter in the machine and two cherries pop up. You receive five quarters as a pay-off. Two are set aside in a separate cup, and the other three are placed in with the $4.75 balance of the session money. This means you have 50¢ in one cup, never to be touched again on that day, and $5.50 as your session money. What it is doing, in effect, is giving you extra money to act as working capital. But since your Loss Limit was 30% ($1.50), you must leave that machine when you get down to a balance of $3.50. When that happens your session is over, and you check your winning cup to see how many coins were accumulated.

Notice the difference in the two methods. The straight method sets a goal. You continue to play at that machine until you reach your loss limit (for example, up to 60%), or hit your win goal (for example 60%); whereupon, you split the winnings, take a 50%

guaranteed profit, and play with the excess. After each win in the excess, you split the take 50-50 with half being added to the guarantee and half added to the excess which is kept in action at that machine until the excess is exhausted.

The Chicken Method operates on the theory of setting lower loss limits, perhaps 30%. But each payoff immediately is split 50-50 with half going to the guarantee cup and the other half staying with the session money.

These are two theories that have worked well through the years, primarily, because of their disciplined nature. Remember, my idea of winning is based on consistency rather than by killings. But the most important part of my theory is that I concentrate on minimizing your losses. That you must learn to do and accept.

# KNOWLEDGE OF THE GAME — SLOTS

## Dollar Machines

In the previous chapters, all of the examples I gave were based on quarter machines. In Vegas you have 5¢, 10¢, 25¢, & $1 slots. While in Atlantic City you have 25¢ and $1 slots with one or two 5¢ ones, just to tickle the urge. Again, since people playing 5¢ and 10¢ slots are probably playing with short bankrolls, they should adhere to the systems shown for the quarter machines, but merely adjust the coins to coincide with their bankroll. The percentages never change—only the amounts.

There is a feeling among 'knowledgable' casino customers that the payoffs on the dollar slots in all casinos are better, percentage-wise, than the quarter ones. Since nobody knows this to be an absolute truth, it will remain a theory until the casinos allow you to examine the percentage pay-off for every machine you play at, before you have to place a coin in it.

Since the chances of that happening are about as remote as my getting a date with the Playmate of the month, you'll just have to take your chances with the pre-set vigorish. With nothing to base these assumptions on, the feeling is that the vigorish on the 25¢ machines, which are played more than the dollar machines, may be somewhere in the 13% area. Conversely, the feeling is that the dollar machines are pre-set for about a 92% return, resulting in only an 8% vig.

Naturally, as mentioned earlier, Las Vegas machines in many casinos are set for 95, 96 and 97% returns. That is beautiful. It gives the player a shot at winning, or at least staying in the game, until he does get a hit; then, it is up to him to walk away a winner. But since most people who frequent the casinos are armed with scared money, the dollar machines are considered too high a risk.

There is no intent to condone playing slot machines, and surely no intent to persecute those who do play them. In all cases you are fighting that lofty vigorish that the casinos have going for them. When I show examples on the quarter machines and talk about $5 session money, it is no big problem for you to adjust the percentages to your own original bankroll.

If Iva Lottakash saunters into a casino with $3000 for some heavy blackjack play but wants to exercise her right arm for a few hours on the slots, let her follow the same percentage set-up. I'm not going to send her to the 25¢ machines. She wants the dollar ones.

The $3000 has 20% or $600 designated for one-armed bandit action, and is subsequently broken down into six sessions of $100 each. Miss Lottakash can get a lot of action on the dollar machines by using the same percentages. In this case she merely applies the 60% win goal to $100 instead of $5. The theory doesn't change; it is only the bankroll that determines the total amount of winnings or losses.

You must learn to discipline yourself as to which value table or which size slot machine you compete at, based on your bankroll. Why do you think Manny S. Ugglee has so much trouble getting a date? Because, he keeps competing at a higher level than the bread he has to work with. The poor guy looks like the loser of a one-sided fight with King Kong's big brother, but he insists on chasing only girls who are finalists in the Miss World Contest. If he dropped down to where he belongs, he could probably get lucky; but, I guess that's what dreams are all about.

However, in gambling, unlike girl chasing, the risks are more expensive. You go to the dollar machines with a ten dollar bill as your total bankroll, and you'll wear out a lot of shoe-leather killing time until your bus is ready to leave.

If I were you, who longs only for the sweet sound of a slot machine bell to bang in my ear drums, I'd wait until I had the bankroll to compete at the dollar machines. Then, I would use one of the aforementioned methods of discipline.

(P.S. A few well-placed prayers might also be helpful.)

# 8 KNOWLEDGE OF THE GAME — SLOTS

## Should I Play More Than One Coin?

One of the hardest games to win at in a casino is blackjack. Yeah, I know, you are an expert at the game. I hear that garbage every day. Then I give the braggart 20 questions on the game of blackjack based on which is the best percentage move for a given hand against the dealer's up card, and Mr. "Know It All" is lucky to get nine right, out of twenty. That same dope sits at a blackjack table, sure to get whacked, because of his lack of knowledge, and then compounds his ignorance by playing two and three hands at a time. There's nothing wrong with playing multiple hands if you know what you're doing.

If you play perfect basic strategy, you're fighting only a 1½% vig to the house, which isn't too bad. So playing two hands, as long as you have the bankroll, won't hurt you. In slot machines you are playing a game that is belting you in the gut to the tune of about 10% vigorish. By putting multiple coins in it does not reduce the vigorish against you. It merely puts more money at risk at this same dangerous percentage.

However, you will have more chances of winning because it allows the symbols on the reels to have more combination possibilities. The first coin, naturally, applies to the combination of symbols shown in the middle of the slot window. If three are inserted, you get two additional combinations. Five coins gives you five opportunities of getting a return.

Remember, since you are playing a machine that cannot be conquered based on any degree of intelligent moves, that damaging vigorish keeps pounding away at every coin that is inserted.

On one hand, you get more combinations from which to extract a profit. The drawback is that all important drain on your bankroll. My theory on gambling will always revert to the size of the bankroll determining the amount of bets you are allowed to place. If you follow my advice and restrict your slot play to a percentage of your overall bankroll and then break that secondary bankroll into a series of sessions, you can easily see the small amount of capital you have to operate with.

With that in mind and realizing that you will have this limited playing money, how can you logically triple your outlay? Do you see how important it is to gamble — only when you are financially stable???

I mentioned the theory among professional players that the pay-offs on slot machines are higher when three or five coins are inserted into the dollar machines. That means the lowest vig against the slot player _may_ be when he risks five silver dollars at a time. That doesn't mean I am telling you to pop into one of the casinos and run over to the dollar machines and start pouring in five coins at a time. I am merely making you aware of what the professional opinions are as applied to the chances of your beating the slots.

Most people play the quarter machines because they just can't afford to do otherwise. They play one quarter at a time hoping and praying that the next pull of the handle will be the elusive jackpot. Who can accurately say what is the exact percentage working against the slot player, whether he plays the quarter, half dollar, dollar machine, or even the 5¢ bandit? Who can tell whether it is wiser to insert one, three, or five coins in either the smaller or larger valued slots? Without knowing the exact presettings on those machines, no one can be sure exactly what the vig is.

If you must play the slots, play multiple coins only when your bankroll allows it; otherwise, follow the rules I laid out.

# KNOWLEDGE OF THE GAME — SLOTS

## Who Plays The Slots?

Let's see if I can pinpoint the few categories of people who play slots:

a) Young people
b) Old people
c) Men
d) Women
e) Single people
f) Married people
g) Divorced people
h) High School grads
i) College grads
j) Drop outs
k) Smart people
l) Dopes
m) People with small bankrolls
n) High rollers with hugh credit lines
o) Blue collar workers
p) White collar workers
q) Professional people
r) The casino novice
s) The professional gambler
t) The daily visitor
u) The junket player
v) Casino personnel
w) Casino slot repair men
x) Everybody

Can you find yourself in that list? Of course you can. It's a fun game. Recently, I saw a movie on TV, the name of which escapes me at the moment, and it starred George Peppard. It was about an out-of-space attack that wiped out the whole country, except three men who were trapped in a shelter for several years.

When they finally ventured out to check out the damage, they found that they were the only people left. Anyhow, they finally arrived in Las Vegas, as they moved around the country, and the whole town was deserted, and had been for years. You know what these guys did? They played the slots — running around this casino pouring in the coins they found lying around, and screaming when they hit a jackpot. Of course money had no value, but in all their misery, they found an outlet in the thrill of the slots. It says something about the writers of the show and also about how people look upon these bandits. I thought it was a tremendous message about this in-grown drive we have to conquer the unconquerable.

All types of people play the slots. You think I've never dropped a handful of coins into those bandits? Of course I have, and so do many people who would hate to admit it. It is soooooo easy. And who knows, the next pull on that handle may set off those bells. That's why so many people are drawn to them.

I'll admit that I no longer have the driving urge to beat them, but I will on occasion, take that shot. And it is always with 3% of my overall bankroll. I take the silver dollars, break them into six sessions, and play the 'Straight 60' method. Have I hit any jackpots? Of course, but rarely more than one on any given day. I enjoy the walk on the edge of reality, knowing full well that the chances of winning are reduced to a shot in the dark. The money management methods I show you and that I use keep the the whole exercise in its proper perspective.

The problem with slots is that so many people go

to a casino for the express purpose of just playing those one-armed bandits. Sure, everyone sneaks over to take a crack every now and then. If you make it your whole day in the casino, you'd better wise up.

I read a certain book on gambling where the author made very light of the fact that people played the slot machines so much. His answer was, "Go ahead and play them — You won't win, but you'll have a good time". There's a guy, a self-proclaimed expert, telling people to play a game that you're going to lose at and have fun. He's gotta be operating with half a deck.

If you have fun losing, you ought to check your own level of brain fluid. You will not beat the slot machines. Period. But, since you cannot get people to stop playing them, you can make them aware of money management, discipline, and how they apply to all forms of gambling.

# 10 KNOWLEDGE OF THE GAME — SLOTS

## Summary Of Slots

There isn't much I can give you on this game. No knowledge is involved, but the other facets of the Big Four must apply as in all games of chance.

**BANKROLL.** Since the vig against you is so high, you should reduce your slot bankroll to a percentage of your overall stake. You decide on the amount. I make mine 3% if, and I said **if,** I am going to play that day and the desire only hits me one out of every nine or ten weeks. Set your bankroll percentage at 5%, 10%, or 20%. Anything; but set it small. This way you will learn what restrictions are and how to live with them.

**MONEY MANAGEMENT / DISCIPLINE.** Nobody should gamble unless they know what they are doing and if they can practice money management and discipline. You shouldn't bet on the slots because of the vig. But if you must, do as I have shown. Pick one of the methods I have outlined, work one up yourself, and follow it. Make sure it is played with only a small portion of your overall bankroll, and played with strict discipline.

You will be surprised at how satisfying these controls will become, how you will satisfy your desire for a few shots at the slot machines, and how your losses will become less frightening.

The wins will come. Maybe not in hugh windfalls but in small consistent clusters. And your losses will be controlled. That's the key . . . When you control those losses, you will be able to compete more often, and thus be in the game long enough to receive those wins.

Slot machines . . . The backbone of the casino take and the back breaker for the player. Don't be a chump. Control your play at these bandits.

# 1 KNOWLEDGE OF THE GAME — ROULETTE

## Roulette — What Is It?

This casino games bounces back and forth as both a popular game and an unpopular game. In Las Vegas it does not receive the attention that is given to the game in the European casinos. Yet, in Atlantic City, it is a terrific attraction.

In Las Vegas there is plenty of room at the other tables, and roulette is treated like a poor relative. However, in European casinos this game is almost the national pastime; almost.

It is believed that roulette first reared her beautiful head in France, and like other gambling games, has been handed down through the years and improved upon until it offers the player a crack at the casino's money with an edge in favor of the house, naturally. And this, again, is called vigorish. This time the vig is 5.26% against the player.

The game is played on a rectangular table containing a layout showing the numbers available to bet on, and a wheel with individual slots containing the same list of numbers.

The numbers 1-36 are shown on the table with

each number being either red or black plus the 0 and 00 shown in green on the layout. These green numbers make up the edge in favor of the house.

Outside of the main block of numbers are additional spaces that may be bet on for various groupings of color, high or low, odd or even, dozens and columns. Each bet will be explained separately.

The combinations or possibilities for different wagers is varied and many. It is the playground for all people with lucky numbers, gut feelings, systems, and all the other illogical approaches that go hand in hand with gambling. More systems have been tried in roulette than on any other gambling game, primarily because of the multiple opportunities for various approaches. The bottom line is always the same — the house holds the hammer. It is your job to win a certain amount of money and walk.

First off, the game is handled by a dealer, or as they call them in Europe, a croupier. An extra dealer is used when the table is very busy. His or her job is merely to help stack the chips due to the various colors used.

There is room for six people to sit at a table comfortably and, when crowded, a few more are allowed to make bets with casino chips while standing behind the chairs if they do not bother the seated players.

It's important that you know how to handle yourself at the tables. If you act like you know what you are doing, the casino personnel will treat you with the utmost respect. If you are a wise guy and loud mouth, you'll only irritate everyone around you, and the casino people will make sure you are kept in your place. When you walk up to a roulette table and decide to play, you will notice a small sign on the table that tells you what the minimum bets are. This way you find out if the limits are within your bankroll. Find a seat and place your session money in front of you. Let's say you will start with $100. The dealer will give you a couple of stacks of chips all of a certain color. We'll make it blue. You will be the only person at that table using blue chips. The value of the chips could be anywhere from 10¢, 25¢, 50¢, $1, etc. In Las Vegas the chips could have a small value which is all at the discretion of the individual player. In Atlantic City, since the minimums are higher, the amount placed on the chips is usually 50¢ or $1.00.

The chips used at a certain table have no value any place else. So, when you are finished playing, you must turn the chips back to the dealer at the table where you are playing. She will give you casino chips for the same value. Okay, you've placed a hundred dollars on the layout and the dealer takes it and counts it out in front of her. She then announces to the pit-boss who is in charge of a group of tables that she is making change for $100. You merely tell her that you want 50¢ chips, and you will receive 200 chips, each valued at 50¢. You are the only person at that table with blue chips. This is to allow the dealers to know which bet belongs to which player. The other players will also receive a stack of chips as they buy in. Again, each person is assigned their own color.

To make sure there is no mistake in the value of the chips, the dealer will place a blue chip around the lip of the wheel with a 50¢ marker on it. This lets everyone know that the value of the blue chip is 50¢. You will be reimbursed this amount for every blue chip you turn in to the house.

After the pit boss acknowledges the buy in, the dealer will push 200 blue chips in front of you and announce, "Good Luck". You are ready to play. Even if five different players all have the same number, the fact that the chips have a different color for each player makes it easy to determine which bet belongs to which player.

After the dealer has cleared the chips from the previous spin, she will leave a marker on the winning number until all bets are paid. Since there are so many combinations that could occur, such as columns, dozens, color, splits, etc., the house eliminates all chances of argument by paying each individual winner in turn. When the dealer finally removes the marker from the previous decision, she will tell the players "make your bets, please". You then make all of the bets that you have in mind. The dealer in the meantime spins the ball around the upper lip of the always spinning wheel. Just before the ball starts to slow down, the dealer will announce, "No more bets, please". That is your signal that no more bets can be placed for that spin. Suppose the ball lands in the eight slot. The dealer will announce, "The winner is #8, black, even". Once again, she'll place the marker on top of the eight to show that this is the winning number.

Notice, if you will, the wheel that is used in the game. The same numbers shown on the layout, 1 through 36, are placed around the wheel; and, naturally, are the same color, either red or black, as their coinciding number on the layout. These numbers are not just placed in a wishy-washy fashion. An attempt was made when setting up the games to try and keep the wheel in some type of pattern by alternating each consecutive number. For instance, one and two are opposite each other. So are three and four, five and six, and right down the line. The effort was made to split black and red, alternate low and high numbers, and odd and even digits. A perfect balance cannot be made, but the best possible distribution has been accomplished.

In front of each number on the wheel is a slot where the small ball will finally come to rest, thereby, alerting one and all as to the winning number, color, dozen, high, low, odd, even, or column. The wheel that is used is perpetually in motion. To begin a new game, the dealer will merely remove the small ball from the previous games' pocket and proceed to spin it around the upper lip again, always in the opposite directions on the constant turning wheel.

# 2 KNOWLEDGE OF THE GAME – ROULETTE

## Roulette – The Layout

I've shown a picture of a roulette layout and will explain the various payoffs on each available bet. Check with the picture and compare the description with the applicable part on the chart.

a) **STRAIGHT UP.** Pays 35-1 and you may place a chip on any one of the 38 numbers on the layout. There is one way to win and 37 numbers that could beat you. So, true odds are 37-1. This is what the payoff should be. The difference between what you are paid and what you should be paid is the house vigorish. In roulette, outside of the five number bet, it is always 5.26 against the player.

b) **SPLIT.** Pays 17-1 and you get two numbers by placing a chip on the line that separates any two numbers that are right next to each other on the layout. Remember, this does not mean they are next to each other on the wheel. Again, you are fighting a 5.26 vig. Incidentally, if you are sitting at the opposite end of the table from the 0-00, you can make the bet by placing your chip between the 2nd & 3rd dozens.

c) **STREET.** Pays 11-1. By placing a chip on the line

next to the first number in a 3 street pattern, you receive 11 chips for each one you bet, if any one of those three numbers appear. Vig is 5.26%.

d) **SQUARE.** Payoff is 8-1. You receive a cluster of any four numbers in a group when you place your chip directly in the center of the cluster. For example, we show a chip in the center of 8,9,11 & 12. You may take any such grouping on the layout. Vig is 5.26%.

e) **LINE (5).** Payoff is 6-1. This bet limits you to the only five number combination on the table when the 0 and 00 is used, as is the case in most casinos in the U.S. Most Las Vegas and Atlantic City tables have both the 0 and 00 on its layout, as opposed to the European game that contains only the single 0. This is explained in the chapter on vigorish. On this number 5 bet, you receive 0, 00, 1, 2, and 3. The vig in favor of the house is 7.89%, as opposed to all other bets holding a 5.26% edge.

f) **LINE (6).** Payoff is 5-1. You have the opportunity of covering six numbers with a single chip. What you are getting, actually, is two rows of streets, since the 6 line bet covers any group of six numbers that are next to each other. You make your bet by placing the chip in the center of the line that joins two streets and overlaps into the dozens section. In my example on the chart, the chip gives you all the numbers from 31 thru 36.

g) **DOZENS.** Pays 2-1. It allows you to take any 12 sets of numbers out of the three possible combinations. Notice again the way the vig operates, as it is very clear on these type bets. By placing your bet in the second dozen, you get every number from 13 through 24. That gives you 12 ways to win, as opposed to the 24 numbers plus 0-00 that could beat you. The payoff is 2-1.

h) **COLUMN.** Pays 2-1. Again, the same mathematical chances apply. The difference is that on this bet, even though you have 12 numbers working for you, they are now in column order. The vigorish of 5.26% still stands because of the 26-12 edge the house continues to hold.

i) **HIGH OR LOW.** Payoff is even. We have reached the part of the board called the 'Outside Bets'. These final three betting sections are always referred to as outside bets, as compared to all wagers on the numbers contained on the inside of the layout. Naturally, these bets are called 'Inside Bets'. The dozens are also included within the terminology of outside bets, although they are not affected by a rule called "En Prison" which we will discuss shortly. Since the ball will fall into any one of 36 numbers or 0-00, there are 18 chances for a low number; (1-18) to appear, and 18 chances for a high number, (19-36), to show. The payoff is even money, and the house wins all wagers when the 0-00 shows (except if the En Prison Rule is in effect).

j) **RED OR BLACK.** Pays even money, and same explanation applies as to high/low.

k) **ODD OR EVEN.** Pays even money, and again the same possibilities of winning or losing as shown above will apply. All of these even money bets are subject to the usual vig of 5.26, except when the En Prison Rule applies, and then the vig is only 2.70%.

There you have the basic explanation of the

layout which is quite simple. The trick is breaking the game down to the type of wager you enjoy the most and applying the proper money management system.

| | NAME | PAY OFF |
|---|---|---|
| A | - Straight Up | 35-1 |
| B | - Split | 17-1 |
| C | - Street | 11-1 |
| D | - Square | 8-1 |
| E | - Line (5) | 6-1 |
| F | - Line (6) | 5-1 |
| G | - Dozens | 2-1 |
| H | - Column | 2-1 |
| I | - High or Low | Even |
| J | - Red or Black | Even |
| K | - Odd or Even | Even |

# 3 KNOWLEDGE OF THE GAME — ROULETTE

## The Wheel

Briefly, here is some information on the wheel. Every wheel is set up exactly the same and is kept in motion all the time. This takes away the crying on the part of the players that the wheel is not being spun hard enough, or it is being spun too hard, etc. On the wheel the numbers are spread in an effort to separate the highs, lows, reds, and blacks in a mathematically balanced pattern.

For instance, the 0 and 00 are on opposite sides of the wheel. So is the 3-4, 5-6, 7-8, and so on. There are no two black numbers or red numbers side by side. It is not imperative that you memorize all of the positions of the numbers on the wheel or their exact position, but it is very easy to strike a similarity in their approximate area.

For instance, examine a roulette wheel. They're all the same. Once you have acquainted yourself with the position of the numbers, it is the same set up in all casinos.

Place the single green zero at the top of the wheel. Let's say you want to memorize all of the numbers on the left side of the single 0. Just think of two individual numbers, 2 and 19. If you were to place a chip on every even number from 2 through 18 and a chip on every odd number from 19 through 35, you will have covered one side of the wheel.

The other side is exactly the opposite. The numbers on the right side of the single 0 begin with 1 and 20. For instance, every odd number from 1 through 17 and every even number from 20 through 36 is included to the right of the green 0 when it is at the top of the wheel.

As you go along, you will discover that all of the things that seem so complicated have a very basic, logical answer. In this case a player could place a chip on every even number from 2 through 18 and every odd number 19 through 35 and cover a complete side of the wheel. I've seen strong roulette players use a money-management system on this betting scheme many times.

Since the pattern of these numbers are set in the same place on every wheel, I strongly suggest you memorize them. It's not going to help that ball fall into a designated slot, but it will help you to understand the game more fully. Being perfectly aware of every facet of every game you bet on will help make you a better player.

The better you are, the better chance you have of winning. Isn't that what gambling is all about?

# 4 KNOWLEDGE OF THE GAME — ROULETTE

## Vigorish In Roulette

Here, again, I go into vig. If you refer back to the bankroll section you will find the definition of vig. I will go over it again in this section because of its importance. All gamblers must get it into their heads that this is the brick wall they constantly must bang into every time they make a bet.

In roulette, the vig is 5.26% on every single bet you make, except for the 5 number line bet which has a 7.89% clout. In Atlantic City casinos they have adopted the En Prison Rule which is explained in the next chapter. For now, let's concentrate on the majority of wagers that can be placed.

I explained in the previous chapter some examples as to how this vig can be calculated. It is so simple, and yet many people cannot comprehend where the house has this edge. Suppose you wanted to make a bet on the color black. By placing a chip on the layout in the section marked "BLACK" you are betting that the ball will drop into one of the numbers that are colored black. What are your chances of winning? Well, there are 18 black numbers and 18 red numbers plus 0 and 00. So, your chances of winning are 18 numbers as opposed to the 20 numbers that will beat you.

This is where the house vig of 5.26% is constantly working against you. This 5.26% is quite a sizable chunk of percentage to give back to the house. By comparing it to other wagering possibilities in a casino, it is not as dangerous as some.

One time I was talking to a guy about his experiences in the casino, and he admitted that he lost all the time. I told him that playing craps, blackjack and baccarat expertly, gave him only about a 1% deficit against the house, and that his chances of winning weren't that bad. I told him that even roulette gave him a fairly good shot if he had a system of play. Listen to this reply: "Yeah, but by playing slots I don't have to know anything. Even though the odds are against me, I meet a lot of girls at the slots". I was going to tell him that he could meet a lot of girls with a lot less money layout, but talking to a nut like that was like trying to teach my dog to use a knife and fork.

Some people play roulette because they hate the slots and don't understand craps or blackjack. Others flat out refuse to play roulette because they read in books that it is the worst game in the casino for the player. That is absolutely not true. I would rather you played roulette than blackjack, unless you were an excellent blackjack player. You could be fighting up to a 30% vig in blackjack, but you never are bucking more than 5.26% if you play all the combinations (except the 5 number line) and no more than 2.70% with the En Prison Rule on the outside numbers in roulette.

Practically everyone I spoke to about the vig in roulette had a different opinion. None knew the true percentage against them. Most were surprised, some didn't care, and all admitted to a definite lack of knowledge in the game.

The end result is that people really don't understand what vig they are fighting. Those with some knowledge of the vig fail to put it into proper comparisons with the other games.

I've explained that the house vig, not counting the 5 number line bet or the En Prison Rule, is 5.26%. Following is a couple of higher vigs in other games:

a) Big Wheel . . . . . . . . . . . . . . . . . . . . . . . . . . . .16.67%
b) Slots . . . . . . . . . . . . . . . . . . . . . . . . . . . .13%
c) Craps, Hard 6 or 8 . . . . . . . . . . . . . . . . . . . 9.1%
d) Craps, Hard 4 or 10 . . . . . . . . . . . . . . . . . .11.1%
e) Craps, eleven . . . . . . . . . . . . . . . . . . . . . .11.1%
f) Craps, any craps . . . . . . . . . . . . . . . . . . . .11.1%
g) Craps, any seven . . . . . . . . . . . . . . . . . . . .16.67%
h) Craps, two sixes . . . . . . . . . . . . . . . . . . . .13.89%
i) Craps, placing 4 or 10 . . . . . . . . . . . . . . . . 6.67%
j) Craps, field, double on 2 and 12 . . . . . . . . . 5.26%
k) Craps, Big 6 & 8 . . . . . . . . . . . . . . . . . . . . 9.09%
l) Blackjack. If you are not perfect in basic strategy, you could be bucking vigs of anywhere from 10% to 30%. This is all based on your *lack* of knowledge of the game of blackjack.

Well, I'm sure the point I'm trying to make has hit home to all you wise guy crap shooters who laugh at the little old lady playing roulette fighting the 5.26% vigorish. You laugh out of the side of your mouth and nod to your buddy what a dummy she is. Then, you place a $10 chip on the four. The percentage against you is worse than the percentage against the gal over at the roulette table.

Now, I'm not writing a book condoning the extensive playing of roulette, but I am not totally knocking it, especially when it compares favorably with the chances of your winning certain bets at craps, slots, and the Big Wheel. Blackjack is pure suicide for the novice. If a person doesn't know blackjack perfectly, he should make a bee-line to the nearest roulette table before he even considers blackjack.

Ok, you have another dose of information on vigorish under your belt. I hope it is sinking in. Roulette is not the best game in the casino, but it is not the worst.

Think about it. Do you really understand the true meaning of vigorish yet? If not, go back over these chapters until that light goes on.

# 5 KNOWLEDGE OF THE GAME — ROULETTE

## En Prison Rule

As I explained before, the casinos in Atlantic City have included a rule in their game called "En Prison Rule". With the addition of this rule, it causes the vigorish against the player on the outside bets to drop from 5.26% to 2.7%. That is quite a reduction in the edge that the casino has against you.

Primarily, the reason for this move was to encourage more people to play roulette. As I explained in the previous chapter, the vig against the player in roulette is basically higher than the best moves in craps; such as Pass Line, Don't Pass, Don't Come, and placing the six and eight, among other moves.

But, since many people believe roulette to be a game totally designed to wipe out every player, the house has attempted to lure people to the table by relaxing the vig against them on certain plays. The old come on game is naturally at play here. If you can get a person into the store with a "sale" on a certain item, he is probably ripe to buy something at a higher marked up price.

The same is true in this case. With the use of the

"En Prison Rule", the vig on the outside numbers is cut in half. Perhaps the player will be drawn to the table with this break and then succumb to temptation and start playing those parts of the table that have higher vigs. Just like the sale in the local stores where they have the "loss leader". Once the customer is in the store he is likely to buy more items. The casinos know that most players have absolutely no money management and will fall prey to greed every time.

Here's how this rule works, but remember, only on the outside bets of black/red, odd/even, and high/low. You are aware of the fact that if you play black, for instance, and red or green appear on the wheel, you lose. Not so with this rule. If red shows, you still lose. But, in the case of the green, either 0 or 00, you would go into "en prison", and the dealer will place an "En Prison" marker on top of your bet.

Suppose you placed a $5 bet on the color black and the 00 green showed. You would have one of two options. You could either surrender one half of your $5 bet ($2.50), or you can elect to go into prison. In the latter case, the dealer would place an "En Prison" marker on top of your $5 chip in lieu of taking the bet. If on the next decision on the wheel either the color red or green showed, you would lose the bet. However, if black appeared, the color you were originally betting, the "En Prison Rule" would be in effect. The dealer would remove the "En Prison" marker from your chip, and you would have the option of either taking down your bet or letting it ride on the next spin.

What this rule does is reduce the chances of your losing on the 0 and 00. Instead of automatically losing on the 0 and 00 when you are playing these three out-side even money bets, you have a second chance at not losing your money. That's where the vig against you is dropped from 5.26% to 2.70%.

To give you an idea of how good that is, it now presents itself as a better percentage move against all of the plays I explained in the previous chapter; plus it now becomes a better bet than:

   a) any other play on the roulette table ......5.26%

   b) any blackjack player who does not have an absolutely perfect knowledge of basic strategy

   c) craps, placing the 5 or 9 ...............4.00%

   d) craps, buying the 4 or 10 ...............5.00%

   e) craps, betting behind any of the numbers .. 5.00%
      (buying the don't for 5%)

So you see, all of those old wives tales that tell you never to bet roulette are telling you to stay away from a game that has less of a vig against you than many bets at the crap table and that have up to two and three times more clout in favor of the house.

Get smart. Learn what games offer you the percentages that give you a chance of staying in the game. The "En Prison Rule" is designed to help the player. If you like roulette, take advantage of it. In the chapters on money management I shall discuss how to bet. But, for now, learn to store these little tidbits in a place in your brain entitled: "Things to remember".

# 6 KNOWLEDGE OF THE GAME — ROULETTE

## Roulette Table Minimums

You've heard the term table minimum and being a smart gambler you know what it means, simply that you have to play a certain minimum amount of money at that particular table. But do you know what it *really* means? Do you aboslutely know the underlying meaning of table minimums? It is the casino's way of keeping the tables clear.

If there were no minimums set up at the various tables, Edgar Squeezeadime could climb up on a chair at a blackjack table at noon and buy in for $11 worth of nickels and hold that seat all day long. No way the casinos could make any money.

In Las Vegas you can find $2 tables, $1 tables, and even 50¢ tables. Years ago, I had the opportunity to deal a 10¢ roulette game. Do you know what it's like to run a roulette table with ten people screaming in hysterical delight when they hit a corner payoff of 80¢ with a 10¢ wager on a four number cluster? "Wow, we can play another hour with that payoff", one charming grandmother exclaimed as she raked in her bounty.

Same old story, all she really wanted to do was

play. She and her compatriots were having a great time coming to the casino two and three times a week and risking $5 or $6 at the 10¢ roulette game.

The house allowed it, as there was very little action on some weekdays. They let the people enjoy themselves, knowing full well that if they got ahead $10, they'd eventually play it all back again.

Most tables had minimum requirements, and on the strip this was usually the case. In Atlantic City the table minimums are very, very rarely lower than $5, and when you can find a $2 or $3 table, it is usually jammed. So, people either risk their skimpy bankrolls at the $5 table, where they usually go broke, or rush over to the Big Wheel and slots where the vig does them in.

On the one hand, the casinos are right in setting this limit so that their tables are not tied up for long hours by people betting 50¢ and $1 chips per hand. On the other side, most people do not have the proper bankroll when they enter the casino and end up getting whacked in a short period of time because of these stringent minimums. Since the casinos are there to be taken, you can't place all the blame on them. They are merely protecting their interests and investments. I do think that they should have more lower-priced tables so that people with short bankrolls can get the chance to compete, but this will never happen, as thousands of people flock to the casinos every week. In Las Vegas if you are a perfect player, that is you have the Big Four, you have a great, great, great chance of coming out ahead, as the table minimums give everyone a tremendous chance to stay in the game. Just don't let greed get to you, and you will win at these games.

In Atlantic city on over-crowded weekends, the table minimums are pushed up to $10, $15 and higher; and lo and behold, they're filled. The casinos dangle the golden ring and the sheep fall in line.

Where does the real fault lie? Right with you, my friend, right with you. If you refused to play at these higher tables, they'd sure bring the minimums down in a hurry. That won't happen because as soon as the novice hits the inside of a casino, he's hooked. He'd bet his wife, if he could get a return on her pound by pound. People lose all sense of reality, so telling them to refrain from betting would fall on deaf ears.

The next suggestion would be to bring more money—a heavier bankroll. But that's like asking for the "Impossible Dream". Some people just flat out can't afford it. They have scraped together every dime they can. They hold back $13 from their allotted food money budget, put 15¢ in the Sunday basket at church instead of the usual 25¢, play only 37 cards at bingo instead of the usual 57, short the paper boy 15¢ on his tip, and hold back a few dollars on their kids' allowance to get together a bankroll for the casinos.

Then they lump their entire bankroll into their wallet; $60, rush to the casino with dreams of winning $1500, and are destroyed in forty minutes. You think this is an exaggeration? Let me tell you, the only phony part of that story is in the amount this guy expected to win. I said $1500 with his lousy $60. He probably had his sights set on $3500.

People are nuts! The amount of money they take to a casino does not allow them the right to play at these high-minimum tables. The answer is that they shouldn't go. Since that statement will also fall on deaf ears, I will attempt to push on.

Many years ago the casinos had 5¢ and 10¢ slots, and people played them. Next came 25¢ machines; then the dollar slots. Next came three coin, and now five coin slots. People pour their money in and are always gunning for the big, bigger, biggest payoffs. By the time my daughters are old enough to play, the cost of a slot will be a $50 gold piece. And, you want to know something? People will be standing in line to play.

Ask yourself how many times did you hit a jackpot or accumulate $75 in winnings after an hour of play by starting with a lousy $10 in quarters, and pour it back in? Many, many, many, many times, I'll bet.

And how many times did you enter a casino with a bulging wallet containing a $50 bankroll and find nothing but $5 minimum tables? Many times, I'll bet. And, I'll also wager a pittance on the fact that you played anyway, hoping that you'd get hot.

How foolish! How utterly ridiculous. Table minimums are set for a purpose. They are telling you right out that you shouldn't be there. If you're dumb enough to attack them with a short bankroll, be prepared to suffer the consequences. I will give you minimums that you must follow in the money manage-ment and discipline chapters. For now, realize one thing. If you don't have the knowledge or the bankroll, you can't compete. It's as simple as that. You just can't play. Period.

Incidentally, there are two separate sets of

minimums in effect at most roulette tables. For instance, the card displaying the minimum might read:

MINIMUM INSIDE — — —$3.00

MINIMUM OUTSIDE — —$5.00

That merely means that if you wish to bet inside the rectangular lines showing 0 - 00 and 1-36, you must space your bets to wager at least $3. You could bet the entire $3 on one number, or spread it out with 50¢ chips laid out on various combinations.

The minimum of $5 is strictly for the outside bets of dozens, black/red, odd/even, and high/low. These sections call for at least a $5 bet on each separate wager. Since the outside bets with the "En Prison Rule" has only a 2.70 vig, it is not uncommon for some heavy hitters to try their systems in these areas. The table minimums in Las Vegas are much lower, but usually the same stipulation of inside and outside minimums will differ.

A final word about the psychology of the casinos putting $5 minimums on the outside bets — They are well aware that money management is something that most players have absolutely no knowledge of, so they force them to play for higher stakes since it is only a slight edge that the casino holds over the player. They feel that in the long run greed will destroy the dope.

If you do not have at least 30 times the amount of the table minimum, you cannot play that session. No excuses.

## Systems In Roulette

I could not possibly cover all of the systems tried in roulette down through the years. Every mathematical genius with even a passing interest in gambling has attacked the tables with a 'can't miss' system in hand. The tables still boldly stand there, taking on all comers. It is almost unbelievable the thousands of people who work up a system in the comfort of their cellar, or on a living room rug, using a makeshift layout and a box of buttons. They are convinced that they have cracked the magical game of roulette and race to the casinos to put their system into play. Eventually, the table wears them down. And, for no greater reason than the lack of the Big Four.

Roulette is a fabulously popular game in Europe. In fact they have a wheel which contains only the house number 0 as their edge against the player. American casinos have both the 0 and 00, which is why that 5.26% vig scares so many gamblers. But, even with the single 0, the system players have a fight.

There are hundreds of systems available, all with good and bad points. But, the few I'll discuss are, in my opinion, the best way to attack the tables. Maybe you can improve on them, and that is the power of theory, but at least be aware that you must have a plan in mind when you play. Get one or two and stick to them.

# KNOWLEDGE OF THE GAME – ROULETTE

## Martingale System

Let's get right to the most popular system in gambling, and let's put it just as quickly to rest. The Martingale System was invented by a man named Martingale, naturally, and is simply a progression type method. The theory is that when something happens, for instance you lose a hand of blackjack where you are betting $5, the system calls for the wager of $10 on the next hand. As you continue to lose, you continue to double your bet after each loss. That means, assuming you continue to lose, the subsequent bets would reach $20, $40, $80, $160, and so on. The idea behind this betting is that when you do win a hand, you recoup all of the money you previously bet plus a profit based on your first bet which in this case would be $5. The fallacy to this nonsense is that you must lay out so much money for a small return. It works beautifully on the kitchen table when you are risking only ·320 buttons to prove your point. Let's see how tough you are when it comes time to place 320 smackers on the table in the casino after already laying out another combined $315 in previous lost wagers. That's $635 at risk to win $5. Your chances of winning are never better than 50-50.

The casinos also have the old standby in their corner—the table maximum. That means there may be a $500 maximum bet allowed at that table, which prohibits the player with the gigantic bankroll the opportunity to continue his doubling up system until a win does occur. For instance, starting with a $50 bet, Hubie Heavyhitter could continue doubling up until he picked up a victory and, naturally a profit. But, if his progression called for $50, $100, $200, $400, $800, $1600, etc., it would be impossible for him to continue after his $400 loss. The table maximum would take over and cause him to bet only $500. Naturally, this would completely destroy the system. But in the long run and in the logical explanation of this system, one of two things will destroy you: either lack of guts or lack of funds. It is just too chancy to lay out huge bets for small profits.

The final word on this system is simple. This is the most popular and most ridiculous system ever invented. Anyone who logically assumes that something will happen because the opposite has occurred once, twice, or even eight times previously is crazy. In fact, the Little Three completely disagrees with this thinking that is preached by the Martingale System. The Little Three tells you to be aware of trends or streaks in gambling. Believe me, professional gamblers are aware of trends in gambling, and if they see something happening, they are more apt to go with it than trying to outguess it by hoping that the opposite is "due" to occur.

A baby may be due in nine months. That's been proven. Bills are due usually around the first of the month, that's a fact. But assuming that something is due to happen because of no other logical excuse than that it hasn't shown in awhile is just plain hogwash.

The basic premise behind the Martingale is pure craziness. Stop assuming that 'something' will happen. The 'something' that will eventually happen is probably a quick trip to the poor house. This system, and its variations, have crushed more than a few people.

# 9 KNOWLEDGE OF THE GAME — ROULETTE

## Mini-Martingale

Still on the subject of the Martingale, you will notice I include it in the section entitled 'Knowledge of the Game' and not in 'Money Management'. That is because most people think that they have discovered the greatest invention of mankind when they try to tell me of this dynamite method of play. It is simply another variation of the progressive style of play.

The drawbacks are always the same. You must risk too much money to win a little. But, as I have stated over and over, the biggest fallacy is assuming that something is supposed to happen because it is due. That's garbage. Nothing is *supposed* to happen. That's why they have a word called "streaks".

You remember back to The Little Three where we alerted you to be aware of trends in gambling. Well, the Martingale, in its own way, is telling you that streaks don't occur or that when they do, it's an occasion that should be looked upon as odd and players should bet for the opposite to occur. Ridiculous.

Willee Ritemore is a regular patron at every roulette table ever built. He comes armed with pen and pad and writes, and writes, and writes. He is keeping tabs on all the patterns of numbers, columns, odds and evens, blacks & reds, everything. When he sees 5 reds come in a row, he rushes over and bets black, assuming that black is supposed to come because it has been dormant for several spins of the wheel.

If red appears, he doubles his bet on black with the explanation that the chance of black coming has now improved because red has shown six times in a row. Unfortunately, the little ball has no memory and doesn't have the slightest idea what has come before. If, indeed, red has the gall to come up for a seventh consecutive time, Willee will now bet 4 units on the next spin. If he wins, he gets back eight units minus the seven he lost on the previous losses, and starts patting himself on the back.

If the red does show for the eighth straight time, Willee stops betting. He limits his bets to three spins, called a mini-Martingale. Agreed, the losses are small and the theory basically has some merit based on the true percentages of six, seven, and eight happenings occurring in succession.

But, look at the illogical end of this system. Any time that a two-decision happening is looked upon as a 50-50 proposition, it is meant that it will end up red or black, odd/even, over an indefinite number of spins, or an unspecified amount of time. It doesn't necessarily mean it is supposed to occur on a red/black/red/black/ red/black type of pattern. It merely means that sometime in the future the two decisions will end up occurring a like number of times. Maybe it could be in the year 2187. Are you supposed to base your bets on that premise?

Try flipping a coin in the air where only heads or tails is the decision. It probably won't happen in an even pattern of heads/tails, etc., after 100 flips, but the number of decisions may be close. I'm saying that you will find many streaks occurring. If two streaks of eight of the same kind happened, the advocate of the mini-Martingale could conceivably have lost seven units on two separate occasions. At $5 per unit he would be out $70, and would need quite a few single digit wins to come even.

By cutting his doubling up pattern to a mini series, he does not solve anything. He is working the same premise, but only on a more limited basis, because he is scared it won't work.

It's like the guy who holds his hand over a flame for five minutes must be nuts. "Wow, that hurts", he screams. "Maybe if I just hold it there for two minutes, it won't hurt as much".

No, it won't, but he's nuts just the same. The only question is how big a differential there is between a big nut and a little nut. I think they're equal.

Any type of system where you try and outguess the occurrence instead of using good old home-spun knowledge and logic is a joke. So is the idea of doubling your bet to recoup past losses.

When a trend occurs, it probably will continue to occur for a while. Learn to ride with them, not against the tide.

A touch on how the professional gambler differs with the Martingale Theory is the novice who doubles his bet looking for the trends to change. The pro looks for something to happen and then climbs aboard. Take sports betting. I've heard guys tell me they wait for a team to lose three times, for example, the Yankees. After the Yanks drop three straight games, the novice starts betting with them and doubling his bet. The pro climbs all over the winning team and continues to bet against the Yanks until they 'prove' they can start winning. Players are human, and when they start losing they sometimes get down, and start pressing, and sometimes fall into a bad rut. That's why bookies flourish, just like casinos. One of the main reasons is that old double up when you lose garbage.

# 10 KNOWLEDGE OF THE GAME — ROULETTE

## Crooked Wheel

How can we talk about roulette without touching on the crooked wheel? You've heard these stories before, so let's get right to it. The wheel is not crooked. The wheel's not out of balance, they're not gaffed, or fixed. There is no magnet to draw the ball into the zero & double zero. In other words, there is no hanky panky going on. Does that disappoint you? That means you can't blame your losses on the fixed wheel, only your dopey playing.

I've heard these cry babies who go to a casino three times a year and cry 'fix' if a certain number comes up twice in a row. They see too many movies of the house being able to control where that ball drops. What nonsense.

The casinos don't have to cheat. This is a tough enough game to conquer with a steady 5.26% vig working against the player. The house would be crazy to even consider attempting to cheat.

I don't know why so many people yell 'fix' as soon as things go against them. They don't lose because the house has rigged the wheel against them. People lose because they have either a short bankroll, or they have no knowledge of the game they're playing, or they don't know how to manage their money, or they haven't got the discipline to quit when they're ahead a certain percentage of the money they started with.

*That's* the reason why people lose, and it sounds an awful lot like the lack of the Big Four.

Crooked wheels? Put it out of your mind. That's only for the movies. Try blaming yourself for your losses. You'd be closer to the reason.

# 11 KNOWLEDGE OF THE GAME — ROULETTE

## Summary On Knowledge

Actually, there is really no knowledge attached to the game of roulette. It is merely an attempt to offset the vig of either 5.26% inside, or 2.70 outside when the "En Prison Rule" is in effect.

Now, if you wish to play the game, it is your job to beat the house vig; admittedly, the biggest obstacle in gambling.

In the following chapters on money management, I will lay out several systems for use at the table. I find these to be the most useful, mostly because they are geared to minimizing losses, which is the key to gambling. As long as you keep your losses down, you will have money to play with. The wins are not necessarily supposed to be gigantic, and you'd better remember one basic item. Even with all the knowledge in the world, you still only have a little less than a 50-50 chance of winning. Realize that, and you will be glad to take the small profits.

Knowledge of the game — number 2 on the Big Four list. It is only 25% of the whole package. Even as simple a game as roulette must be understood perfectly.

have you memorized the entire wheel where you know which numbers are on the right side of the 0 and which are on the left? Maybe, down the road, it'll help you win a measly ten bets at $5 a pop. Considering it will save you losing those ten bets, that's a swing of $100.

No reason not to be perfect. If you really want to learn how to win — then learn everything you can about whatever you gamble on.

# 1    MONEY MANAGEMENT

## Money Management—What Is It?

Ah, here we are—money management. Do you know what money management is? Do you practice money management? If the answers to both questions are "No", then you are probably getting whacked at gambling. This is the third step in the Big Four. While it is still only 25% of the whole ball of wax, it does have its own prominent importance.

All casino players talk about money management, yet few practice it. Why? Because it's too hard, it takes too much concentration, it's too restrictive, and they don't know how.

All types of excuses, and yet all are true. Since bankroll is the starting point of the Big Four and determines the amount of wins and losses, so, too, does money management figure so tightly in your play. You can have thousands of dollars as a bankroll. If you don't know how to manage it, you'll still end up a loser.

When I tell you that money management is restrictive, you'd better believe it. It almost chokes you, yet that is the way it must be. It is very hard to force yourself to stay within the guidelines of the conservative style that is required to be a consistent winner. It is the lack of this willingness to be controlled that destroys most bettors.

If you're not going to listen to my suggestions on money management, you may as well close the book right now. You're kidding yourself if you think this facet of the game can be overcome because you have a heavy bankroll and know the game inside out. Money management is the wheel that turns the motor that allows you to reach the ultimate goal — victory.

Since I do not want my bankroll put at risk at the first table, I take the total bankroll that I take to the casino and break it down into three separate sessions. This prevents me from losing all or most of my starting bankroll at the first table. I use three sessions as my three separate attacks at different tables. In this case, I will take one third of my money to three different roulette tables.

A session can be any percentage of your total bankroll. I use three. Suppose you bring $300 to the casino. You now have three separate sessions at $100 apiece. When you walk up to that first table, you will buy in for only $100 in chips. The other $200 is kept aside to start any future session you may need.

Here's how you figure the amount to start a session. The casinos will display a card on each table showing the minimums that are allowed in each game. Usually in Atlantic City the minimums are $3 inside and $5 outside. In Las Vegas the minimums are lower, so a $100 buy in will always be sufficient. With the higher minimums in Atlantic City, you want enough of a bankroll to allow you to play comfortably.

Check out the inside table minimums and multiply it by 30. You must always have at least 30 times the amount of this minimum at that particular table. In this case a $3 inside bet, times 30, is $90 and is within the required amount. If you wish to play the outside bets with the systems I will give you, then you need 30 times $5 or $150 per session. That means your starting bankroll should be $450.

Check out the following chart:

INSIDE MINIMUM  — — — — — — — — — — — —$3.00
REQUIRED AMOUNT PER SESSION   — — — —$90.00
REQUIRED BANKROLL  — — — — — — — —$270.00
OUTSIDE MINIMUM  — — — — — — — — — —$5.00
REQUIRED AMOUNT PER SESSION  — — — —$150.00
REQUIRED BANKROLL  — — — — — — — —$450.00

Naturally, if you are going to play an inside system, you don't have to worry about what the outside minimums are.

Money management is knowing every single, solitary move to make at an instant's notice. The following chapters will elaborate on the loss limits and win goals. But right now, it is imperative that you realize the importance of money management.

# MONEY MANAGEMENT

## 2

## Scared Money

Come on, you know what it means. It means just what it sounds like. People bring money to the casinos and they are scared that they're going to lose. I mean petrified. It might be the rent money, food money, extra money for the kids' college, or any number of things. Many people go through the trauma of betting money that should be put aside for more important things. But the lure of gambling and the promise, or hope of big killings, cause people to use this scared money not only in the casinos but on lotteries, bingo, races, sporting events, cards and all sorts of wagering.

The fact that the bettor is aware that he is betting with the bottom of his available cash causes him to bet irrationally or scared. He will allow this small bankroll to dictate how he bets. He will be afraid to bet in the manner that is required, and will probably not be able to take advantage of hot streaks because of his scared approach.

You think there isn't a lot of scared money being bet in the casinos? Think again; you can spot the players a mile away.

Some woman loses five straight quarters in the slot machines, and acts like she just lost the mortgage on her house. The loud mouth at the crap table has just sevened out. He turns his back to the table and counts his chips three more times. He still has only seven chips left. Watch him. In the next three minutes he'll count those seven chips 14 more times as though they will magically double in his sweaty palms.

Over at the blackjack table, Vedy Shortkash has lost three straight hands at $5 a pop, and screams to the pit boss that he thinks he's being taken by the quick fingered dealer, who incidentally, is dealing out of a shoe. It is simply that he cannot afford to lose three hands. His total bankroll for the day was $65. No wonder he's screaming.

And finally, we slide over to the roulette table. Two guys betting 25¢ chips between them are threatening to call in the casino control commission, as they think the wheel is rigged because the color black came up four times in a row. (They were betting red).

You think these are isolated cases? Think again. These people are absolutely devastated when they lose a few dollars. That is why I want you to bring enough money with you to allow a freedom of worry if you happen to lose a few dollars.

It doesn't mean you will bet the entire amount you bring. But it will allow you to play comfortably. Don't play with scared money, or even a short bankroll. If you don't have the proper amount of money to give you three separate sessions — don't gamble.

The casinos will still be there when you're ready. Remember the times you had a wallet full of money and went for a day's outing at the casino? You lost for awhile, but you were able to stay in the game and finally your streak came. You won back the $600 you were down, and picked up an additional $700.

The hazards of betting with scared money were never evident in those days. Be smart; bring all the tools that are required to play sensibly.

# 3 MONEY MANAGEMENT

## Money Management — Who Needs It?

If you bet on anything at all—cards, craps, horses, slots, bingo, lottery, sports, roulette, you name it—you need money management. In the front of this book I outlined a money management system in slots. You think that's crazy? Let me explain the theory behind money management. Money management does not help you beat a game — it only manages your cash. I didn't tell you that the money management methods that I outlined would guarantee you constant wins. What it does is control your bets and, if you follow the systems to the strictest point, you will minimize your losses. As long as you keep your losses to a minimum, you will have money to play with.

Then, when you get ahead with a streak of wins, you will be able to walk away a winner if, and I said if, you are able to practice discipline. You see, the Big Four covers every facet of gambling that you will come up against and puts it under control. It looks at gambling intelligently, by restricting your losses and getting you to accept small wins.

The housewife who dabbles in the daily lottery at the corner store is our next subject. If she is able to set aside $8 a week for taking a chance on the lottery, she shouldn't put it all in action on the first day. Then if she loses, she is out of the game for the rest of the week.

What she should do is manage her money to a point where she has X number of picks going each day. This doesn't guarantee her a win, but it does keep her in action. It is a simple case of money management.

Lemmy Bettquik walks up to a roulette table, buys in for $200, and starts spreading his bets all over the table. For a half hour or so, he fluctuates back and forth, winning some, losing some. All of a sudden, he hits a dry spell of two or three wipe-outs. Since he had bet approximately 25% of his entire bankroll on each spin of the wheel, this small run of three losses practically wiped him out.

Now he is down to about 30 chips and starts betting scared trying to stay in the game and make his few chips last until it's time for the bus to leave. He was looking for the quick scores that would allow him to play comfortably all day, but he doesn't take into consideration that the wheel could go against him in the beginning and take away what he needs to compete — money.

If Lemmy would learn to bet small and manage his wins and losses in a controlled fashion, he would be able to last longer. The desire to bet large amounts is ingrained in many small bettors. You must have a controlled system of increasing and decreasing your bets based on the previous decision, not on gut feelings. The smartest player needs money management, so does the dumbest, richest, poorest, the novice, and the professional.

Everyone needs money management — everyone.

# 4 MONEY MANAGEMENT

## Theory Of Money Management

I've taken my share of lumps in a casino, and most of it was due to a lack of money management or discipline. So many times I would be ahead and then pour it all back in. I was always looking for the kill — much like you are right now. Admit it. When you go to a casino, your thoughts are not 'Will I Win', but 'How much will I win?' There's a difference. That's why the term "Learning To Win" does not mean learning how to play. It means just what it implies. You must learn how to get ahead and then learn to walk away a winner.

Years ago, after finally realizing that my approach to gambling must have flaws in it since I was winning a lot but never walking away a winner, I devised this regression system. The first thing you must realize about gambling is that no matter how smart you are, no matter how much you know about the game, your chances of winning are rarely better than 50-50.

For instance, I am an expert player in baccarat, craps, roulette and a car counter in blackjack. I have a bankroll, money management and discipline. I don't win all the time.

Well, why don't I? If I'm so smart, how come I don't win every time I sit down at a table? The answer is very simple; very logical. Even with all of my knowledge, my chances of winning are still 50-50, and that's being a perfect player.

If you're not perfect, how can you expect to consistently get ahead? And if you don't have a money management system, you'll be making bets in a haphazard method with no set pattern in mind.

I've seen people at a roulette table make their bets on numbers based on how far they can reach from the spot where they are sitting. What does that prove? Simply, that if they were in another spot at the table, they would bet the numbers that they could reach from that station. And that's supposed to be a method of playing? All these people are doing is allowing the luck of the seat they have determine the placement of their bets. There is no intelligent game plan attached to their play. Eventually they'll get hurt.

The theory or approach to gambling should have a method or meaning for every bet you make. Money management, being the third let of the four-prong ladder of the Big Four, reflects the section of the Little Three called "theory". How you bet is your theory as to how to manage your money. If you have no hard and fast rule for making a succession of bets at a roulette table, then that means you don't understand what money management is. You have no theory as to how you will attack that particular game or session. That means you have no direction, and ultimately you will get whacked.

I have several theories on how to control your session money. They are my theories, and they work. Naturally, you won't win all the time. That's impossible. As you become more proficient at roulette and other casino games, you will get to understand the importance of money management and develop your own systems and methods of control. It will be your opinion as to how to handle your money — it will be your theory.

# MONEY MANAGEMENT  5

## Money Management At Roulette

In the next couple of chapters I'm going to show you some systems to use at roulette. They are designed to keep you in the game, to minimize your losses, and to give you solid methods of play at this game. Roulette systems run into the hundreds, but the ones I will show you are designed to put a lid on heavy losses and get you ahead. Whether you walk when you're ahead or not is strictly up to you.

But even if you perfect the few systems that I will give you, you'll be wasting your time, unless you accept the money management controls that are essential to winning. You wanna be a big shot at the tables and act like money means nothing to you, that's your problem. If showing off is your bag, live it up. But if you wanna win, follow the rules. The choice is yours.

A roulette table is no different than any form of gambling. You need the Big Four. That means that your bankroll should be broken into three sessions with each session providing enough money that would allow you to bet comfortably. Don't worry, with your loss limits to protect you it is impossible to lose all the money in your session.

But, to play with a relaxed, confident air you must have 30 times the amount of your first bet at the table. Let's say you use one of the systems I suggest and it calls for an initial layout of $8. For that session you should have 30 × 8, which is $240. That calls for $720 for an overall bankroll.

If your first bet and each bet thereafter in a session calls for a $5 wager, you must have 30 × 5, or $150 per session and $450 for your starting bankroll. The money management part comes after you divide your bankroll into three sessions. Some people will claim they don't have the time to be bothered by money management. And it's true. You get involved in the game at hand. Control seems the furthest thing from your mind.

Well, you'd better straighten out your entertainment buds. When you walk up to a roulette table, you'd better be there to win. And get that garbage about playing for fun out of your head. It's war, baby.

Notice that the money management section of roulette contains the systems of playing, instead of being placed in the section entitled Knowledge of the Game. That is because roulette is a gigantic game of money management, and ties in very closely with knowledge.

I am going to give you only five systems. The variations off of the basic play can encompass over fifteen different approaches, for each system. That is why I don't want to fill your head with systems that you will never use. Pick a couple of the following, master them, and then lay out your variations. These are the systems that will be covered:

1. Regression System
2. D'Alembert System
3. Labouchere System
4. Action Number System
5. Multi-Numbered System

Each of these systems will be shown separately. Get to understand the theory behind each of them. As you progress in your knowledge of roulette, you will be able to work out methods of combining one system with the other. For instance, the Regression System can be applied to the Action Numbered System, with both methods lending a portion of their theory to the final variant. Read on.

# 6 MONEY MANAGEMENT

## Regression System

You are aware that gambling, at best, gives you a 50-50 chance of winning. Naturally, you always want to bet on something that you know a lot about, and something that offers you the least chance of losing.

At the roulette table, the outside bets consist of black/red, odd/even, and high/low. They are called even money bets, since they return an equal amount of money as reflects the amount you bet. If you bet $5 on black and black comes in, you receive even money, or $5, as your winnings.

There are 36 numbers on the layout consisting of 18 red and 18 black. Since the house could not expect to show a profit if they allowed the patrons a 50-50 chance of winning, it is the inclusion of the two green numbers, 0 and 00, that gives them the edge.

That means if you bet on black, you have 18 ways of winning and 20 ways of losing: the 18 red, and the two greens. As I explained earlier, this gives the house an advantage of 5.26 in their favor.

To stimulate interest in roulette, some Las Vegas casinos and mostly all of the ones in Atlantic City have come up with the En Prison Rule, which lowers the vig to this 2.70 figure, but only on the outside or even money bets. Now, the trick is how do we take advantage of it?

First your bankroll should be divided into three separate sessions and each session started with a comfortable amount of money. To play on the outside sections where the minimum is $5, you should have 30 times the amount of the minimum at that table. If the minimum is $5, then 30 × 5, or $150, should be your session money. That means your bankroll should be $450 for that day.

Your first bet is $10. If it wins, you take back the $10 you won, and regress your original $10 bet back to $5. If you lose that second bet, you still have the $10 you won and one half of your original bet of $10. You have $15 sitting in front of you. Since you started with $10, your profit is $5. The theory of this method is that you can win a bet, lose a bet, and still show a profit. In this case, $5.

To rehash it, you enter a casino with $450 which is your bankroll. You split it into thirds, and have $150 per session. When you sit at a roulette table, you buy in for $150 which is your session. As soon as you make that first bet, it is called a series. The series will continue to be alive until you lose. At that point, the series is over, and you begin the next series with another $10 wager. The series I just explained about ended as soon as the loss occurred, but it showed a $5 profit even though you only played the casino to a stand-off in two spins of the wheel.

The next series begins when you take a $10 bet from your session money and place it on the table.

Let's assume you are playing black. If red appears, you lose, and that series is over. You start with another $10 to begin another series. If you lose four straight series in a session, leave that table, as the trend is against you. So you kill the session, and walk away.

OK, you place $10 on the color black which means a series has started. The balls drops into the slot of #2, black. You win $10, and this series is now alive. When it does end, you are guaranteed to have a profit for that series. The amount of the profit will depend on how long a winning streak can be maintained. But the profit for that series is assured, due to the fact that you reduced the money at risk for the second spin of the wheel after the initial win.

When the dealer pays you off for the $10 win, you pull back that $10 plus one half of your original bet. Keep it in another stack in between your bet and your session money. This lets you know that a series is alive. Psychologically, you will get a lift, even after you eventually lose on a series, since the money in that extra pile will contain your original bet plus a profit, depending on the length of the series. As long as that series stays alive, you will adopt a method of up and pull.

For instance, after you won the initial bet of the series, $10, you regressed to a $5 bet to insure that the series would end up a winner. If you win the second bet, $5, you now have $10 riding on the third spin of the wheel. If you lost, you still have the $10 you started with and a $5 profit.

However, if you win the third spin, you receive a $10 payoff. At that point, you increase your bet by $5, making $15, your wager for the fourth spin, and pull $5 back to your series excess. If you lose that fourth bet, you still have the $10 original bet and a profit of $10. As you continue to win, you remain in that pattern of 'up and pull'.

Each time you win, you go up on your next bet, and you pull back a profit. Since we're still in that winning series, let's assume we won that $15 bet. At this point you have three options. These options should be decided upon beforehand, so that when they occur your money management method is second nature.

You win $15 on that fourth spin, and you either:
a) Pull back the entire $15 to your excess pile, and let $15 ride on the fifth spin, or
b) Increase your series bet to $20, and pull back $10 to your series excess, or
c) Increase your series bet to $25, and pull back $5 to your series excess.

On that fourth wager in the series of $15, a win would give you a payoff of $15. Different theories of money management would apply, depending on the nature of the individual player.

If he was a super conservative player, he might pull back the entire $15 and let $15 ride on the fifth bet. If he was fairly aggressive, he would increase his wager for the 5th spin to $20 and pull $10 back for his excess. That means if he lost that $20 bet, he'd show a profit of $20 for that whole series.

The final option is of an aggressive nature whereby he increases his bet for the 5th spin to $25, by adding $10 to his series bet and pulls back $5 profit for his series excess. Even if he loses that $25 bet on the fifth spin, he has his original bet back and a $15 profit for the series. In no event should he increase his bet for the fifth spin by the entire $15 he won on the previous decision. He is then defeating the theory of 'Learning How to Win'. In that case, he would win $15, and let it all ride on the next decision. That's foolish.

The method of Up and Pull guarantees an increase in the next bet and an increase in your series profit. For the newcomer to this system, I would suggest a repeat of the $15 bet for the fifth spin. That would give you a profit of $25 for that series. Suppose you lost on that fifth spin. The series is over. A $25 profit is placed with your session money, and $10 is put on the layout to begin a new series. That succession of bets ran as follows: Get yourself a handful of chips and follow through with the example.

Ex. 10 - 5 - 10 - 15 - 15 (lost on fifth roll and series is over). Profit of $25, but you were guaranteed of some profit after that first win.

It breaks down like this:

|    | BET  | DECISION | PULL | BET ON LINE |
|----|------|----------|------|-------------|
| 1. | $10  | W        | $15  | $ 5         |
| 2. | $ 5  | W        | —    | $10         |
| 3. | $10  | W        | $ 5  | $15         |
| 4. | $15  | W        | $15  | $15         |
| 5. | $15  | L        | —    | —           |

Above, I've shown you a table on a possible regression grouping. In this series, even though you lost $15 on the last bet, you get your original bet of $10 back plus end up with a $25 profit for the series. Staying with this same series, take a look at where you stand after the first win. When that first decision was in the bank as a win, you were guaranteed a profit for that series. No matter what happened on any succeeding spin of the wheel, you were sure that a profit would be realized. And that is the power of this system.

Next look at the variations. Anywhere down that table after the first win, you had options as to how much or how little would be your next bet. For instance, on bet #3 you bet $10 and won. On the next spin of the wheel you bet $15. You could have repeated the $10 wager. Naturally, as you continue in a series and reach the fifth and higher levels of bets, your variations become greater.

For now, try and understand the basic idea of the method. I also call this the New York System, since the bets are usually in units of 2-1-2 which is New York's area code.

# 7 MONEY MANAGEMENT

## Theory Of Regression

This system works because of the basic theory behind which it operates. That is, you could win a hand, lose a hand, and be ahead of the house. It is not easy to win at gambling if you do not have the Big Four. I've said it over and over again, mostly to get to the people who are too dumb to realize that they are losing because of a lack of one, two, or even three of the categories of that Big Four.

In the New York System, after you win the first decision of a series, you have locked up the profit as soon as you regress to a lower amount. Naturally, you will be betting higher than the amount of the second bet in order to be able to drop back to this lower figure.

I have written a book on blackjack called "So You Wanna Be A Gambler", the same title as this book. The color of the cover is different, but the approach to the game is the same since it is all gambling. The New York System is detailed in that book since blackjack, with the perfect appliance of basic strategy, is an even game. And this system works on even games. That's why I suggest you use it on the outside wagers of the roulette wheel. You are in about the same win possibility of a blackjack player. In roulette you are bucking 2.70 with the En Prison Rule. In blackjack you are fighting about 1.60 if you are perfect in basic strategy. Since they are almost equal in the vigorish that you will have against you, both games could be played with the use of this money management system.

Let's examine a possible occurrence at the tables. Four guys walk up to the roulette table with the intention of playing the outside sections. They each place $10 on the color black. Black shows and each participant wins $10. But each has a different theory as to how to bet the second spin of the wheel.

Player A — Pulls back his $10 winnings and lets original $10 ride.

Player B — Pulls back $5 and lets $15 ride.

Player C — Plays aggressively and lets the whole $20 ride.

Player D — Uses the New York System, pulls back $15, and leaves $5 in play for the next spin.

On the next spin of the wheel it shows red, and all four players lose.

Player A — Lost his $10, and ended up even.

Player B — Lost his $15 bet, but since he pulled back $5 after his first win, ends up a $5 loser.

Player C — Let his original bet and $10 win all ride, and ends up a $10 loser.

Player D — Loses his $5 bet, but since he took back $15 after the first win, he has his original $10 bet back, plus a profit of $5.

Notice that all players won a hand and lost a

hand. In other words, they played the table even, which is what is supposed to happen in a 50-50 proposition bet. Yet, each player had a different amount of money left after the series ended. The New York System held the house to a standstill and ended up with a profit after the completion of the two hands. No other theory showed a profit.

Now, the cynics will argue that the results would be different if each player won the second hand. Granted, but now you're assuming that you are going to win more hands in a row — all the time. This person keeps shooting for the big score, unable to understand how important it is to minimize losses. My system overcomes the chopping table where a player wins a hand, then loses, then wins, then loses, with no streaks showing.

The guy who plays even by continually pulling back the same amount that he won, never gets to take advantage of the streaks, which is mandatory if you expect to make your profit and quit.

Since all methods of money management have a plus and minus, the only drawback to this system is the fact that you must bet higher on the first bet than the table minimum. The guys with the short bankroll and scared money will hesitate to lay out this amount. That's why I insist that you have a bankroll when you enter a casino.

Going to the tables with a total bankroll of $80 is pure suicide, especially with high minimums in effect. You're not going to win consistently enough to offset the times that you get wiped out in a hurry.

In Las Vegas the table minimums are such that

you can stay alive longer in order to take advantage of those streaks that will come. Using this system on a Vegas roulette wheel with low minimums of $1 will help the player who is going in with a small amount of money.

The people with the decent bankrolls will be able to lay out the proper bets. Since most people go into the casinos short, I am talking to most of the people about what is needed. If you're not listening — it's your loss.

# 8 MONEY MANAGEMENT

## Variations Of Regression

You are aware of what the theory of this method is, and it's very simple. After your first winning wager, merely reduce the amount of the second bet. That locks up a profit, as you will always be betting less on the next hand than you won on the first. So the profits aren't gigantic. Well, then, get yourself a hefty bankroll, and you'll be able to bet in tune with your greedy dreams.

This system allows you to take advantage of streaks, offset a chopping table, and minimize your losses by giving you constant profits on one and two victories in a row.

Let's get to variations and a subject many players don't understand. When you see a table marked 'Five Dollar Minimum', that means your lowest bet has to be at least $5. That doesn't mean that every single bet has to be in increments of $5 chips. When I play at a $5 table, I make sure to get $1 chips, which allows me to vary my bet, depending on trends and patterns. There's nothing written in the rules that say you can't bet $8, $17, or $26 on a spin of the wheel or hand of blackjack.

I've had a lot of people admit that they didn't

know that you could wager in off amounts. They thought that each bet over $5 had to be $10, $15, $20, $25, and so on. Using this regression system, just like any money management method, calls for a bankroll. If you don't have a bankroll, you shouldn't be even thinking of playing. And I've said that enough times, that by now it should have sunk in.

For those of you who have a short supply of money to gamble with — incidentally, I am talking to the majority — I suggest you start with lower amounts. Many casinos have $1 and $2 minimums on the outside plays of roulette so you need only start your first series a notch or two above that minimum. In Atlantic City you'll find that the weekends bring big crowds, and the minimums of the outside bets are jumped to $10 and $15 a pop. Where is the short bettor going with a lousy $100 in his kick? Nowhere!!! One short, bad trend and you're sitting on the bus, trying to kill five hours until departure time.

First, I insist that you go to the lowest possible minimum table you can find. Maybe it's a $3 table, and you'll feel embarrassed. So what? You're not there to impress anybody. Maybe the girl you took to the casino thinks you're a big spender, so you try and impress her with gambling stories that always have you dealing in telephone numbers. Come off it! The guys who win and lose big amounts have to have it to bet it.

Let's say you find the $3 table. Put the system into play with varying amounts of bets, a few dollars higher than the minimum. In this way, after a win, you can always drop back to the lower start. This doesn't mean you're locked into betting dollar chips all the time. It just allows you to get a cushion for the bigger bets later on; and, if you catch a cold wheel, your losses are held down.

I'll give you a sampling of bets to be made at tables showing minimums of $3, $5, and $10. Remember two things. You should have at least 30 times the amount of the table minimum to play a session. And secondly, this system should only be used on the outside sections of the table. Your own personal bankroll will help you determine which series to follow.

The series begins with the first bet and continues as long as you keep winning. As soon as you lose, the series is over, and you start a new series with the same amount of the bet that you started the first series. If you lose the first bet of your first four series, the session is over, and you move to another table. Don't fight the bad trends. If it is going bad for you at a certain table, it could continue to go bad for a long, long time. Simply move to another table and begin another session.

### THREE DOLLAR TABLE
(Should have $90 per session and $270 bankroll)

|         | A    | B    | C    | D    | E    | F    |
|---------|------|------|------|------|------|------|
| 1st Bet | $5   | $5   | $6   | $7   | $7   | $8   |
| 2nd Bet | $3   | $3   | $3   | $3   | $3   | $3   |
| 3rd Bet | $5   | $6   | $5   | $6   | $6   | $9   |
| 4th Bet | $8   | $9   | $9   | $10  | $10  | $12  |
| 5th Bet | $10  | $12  | $9   | $15  | $15  | $15  |
| 6th Bet | $10  | $15  | $13  | $15  | $20  | $15  |
| 7th Bet | $13  | $15  | $15  | $20  | $25  | $10  |
| 8th Bet | $15  | $20  | $20  | $25  | $25  | $5   |

Notice that the pattern of your bets can be conservative or aggressive, depending on your own personal feelings; but you must have the pattern perfectly in mind before you start the series. Know ahead of time exactly what the next bet will be each time you win. Look at Table F. Notice you can get super conservative to start your regression after you hit a certain level bet. Do you know how hard it is for someone to bet $15 on the spin of a wheel? Very, very hard. Even though they are ahead, some people can't force themselves to bet higher than a certain amount. Good for them. The time will come when you will reach that point. For now, bet what you feel comfortable with. For the beginner, I recommend Table A. It's conservative, and has a repeat bet on Bet #5 and 6.

### FIVE DOLLAR TABLE
(Should have $150 per session and $450 bankroll)

|         | A    | B    | C    | D    | E    | F    |
|---------|------|------|------|------|------|------|
| 1st Bet | $7   | $7   | $8   | $9   | $10  | $10  |
| 2nd Bet | $5   | $5   | $5   | $5   | $5   | $5   |
| 3rd Bet | $7   | $8   | $7   | $10  | $10  | $10  |
| 4th Bet | $10  | $12  | $10  | $15  | $10  | $15  |
| 5th Bet | $10  | $15  | $12  | $15  | $15  | $20  |
| 6th Bet | $15  | $15  | $15  | $18  | $18  | $25  |
| 7th Bet | $18  | $20  | $15  | $20  | $20  | $25  |
| 8th Bet | $20  | $25  | $20  | $25  | $15  | $35  |

I've explained how table minimums are put in to force the player to bet more money. I've given you several examples which show varying degrees of bets. There is also room for regression, as in 'F', where you start back down the ladder after you have reached a certain point. Naturally, this regression process can begin anywhere in your betting series. I would suggest 'C' for the average player with $150 session money and $450 overall bankroll. Make up your own series. Decide on one which you will feel very comfortable. Following is the $10 table set of runs:

### TEN DOLLAR TABLE
(Should have $300 per session and $900 bankroll)

|         | A    | B    | C    | D    | E    | F     |
|---------|------|------|------|------|------|-------|
| 1st Bet | $13  | $15  | $15  | $15  | $20  | $20   |
| 2nd Bet | $10  | $10  | $10  | $10  | $10  | $10   |
| 3rd Bet | $14  | $15  | $15  | $15  | $15  | $20   |
| 4th Bet | $18  | $15  | $20  | $20  | $25  | $30   |
| 5th Bet | $20  | $20  | $20  | $30  | $25  | $50   |
| 6th Bet | $25  | $25  | $30  | $40  | $40  | $50   |
| 7th Bet | $25  | $30  | $40  | $30  | $50  | $75   |
| 8th Bet | $30  | $35  | $50  | $20  | $60  | $100  |

If you're playing at a $10 table, I assume you have a decent bankroll so the series becomes much more aggressive. This does not rule out the odd amount bets, and I think you will learn to use those 'off' bets to your winning advantage. For example, you could change Series D above to include 'off' amounts as follows: $15 — $10 — $13 — $22 — $28 — $35 — $35 — $33. The variations are innumerable.

One final note on these series bets. If you make up your own series, try to add a 'repeat' bet somewhere along the line. I usually put a repeat in my series about the third or fourth decision. It reinforces the series, and helps keep the discipline factor under control.

# MONEY MANAGEMENT 9

## Regression Options At $25

Ever see the hot shots at a table? Nothing less than winning the east wing of the casino would please them. They never know when to level off their bets or when to pull back a profit. Every word out of them is geared for the "Big Kill". When they win a bet, you can hear them on the next floor "Press It!!!" That's all they know. Keep pressing up the bet. They could win six bets in a row, and they keep screaming "Press It". It's important to them that every person around knows that he's a free wheeler and a big spender. Let him lose a hand after he's increased his bets to the maximum at the table. He yells louder than ever, bemoaning his rotten luck. Incidentally, pressing means you want the bet you won put in with the amount you had at the table without taking a profit.

These guys can't help but go broke most of the time. But it gives them a great story for their buddies while they're all sitting around telling casino war stories. They like to tell about the $5000 bet that went south. I think these jerks are a little wacky inside. If they're not, then they've got bigger problems.

There's a guy I play poker with, I'll call him Ace, but I'm positive he's more an __ __ __ than an ace. He's a fair player but a typical crybaby when he loses, and a big shot when he wins. In other words, a typical dope. Anyhow, old Ace went to Atlantic City about four months ago with about $500. He had a young lady with him, and pretty soon ended up in the baccarat pit. Soon, he was bombed out of his mind (drunk—to you teetotalers), and started betting quite heavy. He caught a bank run of eleven straight wins, and parlayed his streak into $27,000. This is more than Ace makes in two years. You don't want to hear the gory details, but our hero left the casino dead broke, out the $500 he brought with him, and after playing back the $27,000 profit, signed a marker for $500 which also went. It's been quite a few months since this happened, but this jerk tells everyone he meets about what happened. He actually sits there like a pompous boob everytime he relates the story. Instead of bemoaning the fact that he was such a jerk by losing all that money back, he thinks he is a hero because he had the 'guts', as he calls it, to pour that money into the game in an effort to win a gigantic sum. Every time we play, old Ace finds a way to turn the talk to his escapade. He really believes he is a big gambler because of that experience. It hasn't hit him yet what a jerk he was.

There are a lot of people at the tables that go through similar nights. They glory in the attention that comes their way from making big bets, instead of concentrating on the business of winning. They do not *Know How To Win*.

There has to be times when an intelligent decision must be made regarding the larger bets. Some people who stiff their local candy store for a 15¢ newspaper three times a week, throw $25 chips around like they were play money. Then they cry crocodile tears if their kid wants to go to the movies.

These same people put 50¢ in the annual Christmas collection at church, then plop a $50 bet on the spin of a roulette wheel and an additional $10 'for the boys' These blow-hards make me sick. The casino personnel read them as the jerks they are, but play up to them, as they are considered 'prime meat'.

I want you to set the maximum bet in a series where you come up with variations. For the $5 bettor, $25 is about where he raises a few goose bumps when it comes time to make such a wager. When you reach this figure, I'd like one of the following decisions to be made:

a) Same bet.
b) Regress one unit at a time.
c) Drop all the way back to the 1st bet.
d) Decrease $10 at a time for each succeeding win.

Check back for a moment to the $5 table from the previous chapter. We'll go to Series F. When you reached a victory on Bet #6 at $25, the next suggested bet was again $25. Assuming you won again, you should have a predetermined pattern to follow:

a) Either start dropping one $5 bet at a time, making your next few bets $20, $15, $10 as you win, or
b) After repeating the $25 bet and winning again, go all the way down to the first series bet of $10. It'll take discipline to do it, but if that $10 bet loses, you'll be relieved. If it wins, you can start coming right back up the progression scale again, or

c) For you aggressive cats, always repeat your $25 win (if you're a $3 player) and then go up a $10 bet each successive win. But $10 per win is enough until you graduate into a higher series table.

Some of this advice will be accepted by the aggressive player, and some won't. Absorb it all. It is called 'Learning How To Win'. The amounts aren't important. Only the fact that you *do* win.

The options given in this chapter are strictly for the player who reaches a certain level in his series and must make a decision. My Opinion??? Until you learn how to win and until you start getting ahead, use "b" above. It doesn't mean you'll stay this way the rest of your life, but it's a good start to firming up your money management.

# MONEY
## MANAGEMENT 10

## Summary Of Regression

Let's wrap up this system with a list of the pertinent factors that are required:

1) Your first wager should always be higher than the one you will regress to.

2) If you lose the first bet of the first four series at the session—leave that table.

3) Make sure you have 30 times the amount of the table minimum.

4) Loss Limit is 50% of your starting session money.

5) Win Goal should be 25% of your starting session money, regardless of what roulette system you play.

6) This regression system should be used only on the outside bets, that means: black/red, odd/even, or high/low.

7) When you walk up to a table, always buy in for one third of your total bankroll. Don't buy in for less. You're only going to lose a maximum of 50% of that session money. But to be able to play comfortably, have a decent amount of session money available. But it must be at least 30 times the amount of the minimum bet.

8) If you begin a session playing black and red, for instance, you cannot switch to odd/even at that table. You must kill your session and go to another table. If the trend is against you at that particular table, don't try to start out-guessing the wheel. Leave that table.

You don't like the restrictions put on your game? Tough!! Learning how to win is an art.

I never told you it would be easy — only that you would be successful.

# MONEY MANAGEMENT 11

## The D'Alembert System

Many chapters ago, I told you that people have been trying and inventing systems at roulette for many years. A lot of these systems work for periods of time and succeed in holding down that ever present vig. The whole key, of course, is that when you get ahead you must quit.

These systems that are tried invariably contain a form of Martingale Theory, whereby you constantly double your previous bet until you win a hand and recoup all of the previous losses. I've already denounced this type of betting; mainly, because of the short bankrolls of most players. One medium-sized losing streak destroys them.

There are other systems that have merit, and I'd like to place a couple out there for you and have you master the one which appeals to you the most. I hate it when I read about systems that are placed in print by some writer who explains the entire method of play and then tells you you're crazy to bet the game because you're going to lose anyhow.

I agree it is tough to win gigantic sums of money at casino games, but it is possible to grind out small wins using the Big Four.

This system, called the D'Alembert, wasn't invented by a man named Smith, hence, that is where it received its name. It has been used in various forms and especially at the roulette tables in Europe for many years.

This isn't a bad system, and you may like to give it a shot. It requires a pad and pencil so as to give you an easy way to keep a record of your past bets. There are different theories, or approaches, spun off of this system. You may even come up with a variation of your own.

The first step is to write down a number which will stand for units or dollars. You adjust your bets according to the number of units that remain on your chart. It calls for you to continually cross off numbers as you win and add numbers as you lose, depending on the decision of the previous spin of the wheel. Here, again, the outside bets in roulette provide the best use of this system, as they are considered even propositions.

Write the number 1 on a pad. That stands for units. Either the unit is worth $1, $5, or $25. It is up to you. It is dependent upon each person's own bankroll. You pick one of the three classifications of even bets on the roulette layout, perhaps black. For this session you will only play black.

Your first bet is the number shown on the pad: one unit. Red shows and you lose. Write the number 2 next to the 1, and bet two units. Again you lose and now you write the number 3 in the column and bet three units. This time you win. You cross out the 3 with the amount of your next bet being two, an amount one unit lower than what you just won. Your chart looks like this:

1   2   3̸

Again you lose. Again write the number 3 on your chart, and bet three units. Black shows. You win three units, and cross off the 3 and bet two units. Again you win. This time cross off the 2 and bet one unit. Your chart now shows:

1   2̸   3̸   3̸

Since the 1 is still showing, you bet one unit, but red shows and you lose. Write the next highest number of units that you bet on your chart, in this case 2, and bet two units. Black shows. You win two units, cross off the 2 from your column, and have only 1 showing. You bet one unit, win, and now cross off the 1 ending this series. Your chart now looks like this:

1̸   2̸   3̸   3̸   2̸   Complete.

You have a profit of five units. Examine how many wins and losses showed for this series. Black appeared five times, and red four. That means you had an edge of only one hand on the house and ended up with a five-unit profit. Luckily, you did not have to place an enormous bet on the table. This was because you never lost more than twice in a row. The theory behind the D'Alembert Method is that when you lose, you only go up one unit. When you win, it is for more units than the previous losing amount. It does not call for a doubling up method as in the Martingale. If you lose the first six straight in the Martingale, you could be out 63 units. If you lose the first six straight bets in the D'Alembert, you are out 21 units. Of course, the Martingale recoups all the losses on one win, as opposed to the D'Alembert, which only returns a win of one unit higher than the previous bet. But here is where the novice does not understand the danger of long losing streaks. A lot of novices believe you "can't" lose seven or eight even-money bets in a row, and base that thinking on their reasons for the doubling pattern.

The D'Alembert, while not infallable, realizes that it is unwise to buck a losing streak and tries to recoup losses — little by little. On the D'Alembert, you must set a limit on just how high your biggest unit outlay may be. You could set it at seven or eight and then cut off the series, take your loss, and start another series at another table. Or, you could cut your series at five units, or even four, depending upon your session money. But most of all you should restrict your losses by setting this limit. This is being realistic. Don't think it is impossible to lose a long string of even money bets in a row. It happens, and will continue to happen. If you like, set a smaller loss limit on your unit outlay. This will allow you to stay within the confines of a safe bet and still allow some leeway on a table going against you.

In the D'Alembert, you always increase your bet by one unit after a loss, and decrease it one unit after a win. This is a bit different than my own 2-1-2 Regression System which has you increasing your bets in a streak. This system is not looking for long streaks, but simply short, quick series which produce smaller profits, but reacts well to a table giving only about a 50% win factor to the player.

Since betting in units could become dangerous, especially in Atlantic City, which has $5 limits on its outside roulette bets, I shall give you a variation method for the player with a short bankroll. The heavier bankrolled players can use units. The smaller ones try and adopt a dollar-betting method, rather than units.

Incidentally, this system could work well for you in Las Vegas where the minimums may be in line with your smaller session bankrolls. In Vegas you will find $1 and $2 tables, where you will feel right at home.

For now, let's put you at a table with a $5 minimum, playing black/red and again this session will be on the black. Write the number 5 on your pad and bet $5. If black shows, you win. Cross off the 5 on your pad, collect $5, and the series is over. You win $5.

To start the next series, again write 5 on a pad and bet $5 on black. Red shows and you lose. In this case, you do not want to bet in units, but only in partials. You write 6 on the pad and bet $6 on black. If you win, you collect $6. Cross off the 6 and have only the 5 showing on your pad. Naturally, you bet $5 on the next spin.

But let's say you lost that $6 bet. Write 7 on the pad, and bet $7. Again you lose, and write 8 on the pad, and bet $8 on black. Again you lose and the system calls for you to bet $9 on black and write 9 on your pad. This time black shows. You win $9 and cross off the number 9 on the series. Your next bet is $8, which is the next number shown on the series. Again black shows. You win $8. Cross off the 8 and bet $7. Your series looks like this:

    5    6    7    8̸    9̸

You get the pattern? Every time you win, you reduce your bet one unit. Every time you lose, you increase it one unit. The thing I stress is a limit on the amount you will set for your highest bet. Since I strongly believe in trends, I surely refuse to fight one going against me. If I'm betting black and red keeps showing, I limit my maximum bet. In this case it could be $10, $11, or $12. My suggestion? Make it $10. That's enough to get a feel of the trends going against you.

It is a type of loss limit, and must be a part of the arsenal you bring to battle.

# MONEY MANAGEMENT 12

## D'Alembert Variations

Again and again and again I will remind you. When you gamble, it is only a 50-50 proposition, at best. So stop looking for the pot of gold at every session. This system, like all systems, provides you with a money management technique, not a key to the vault.

If I can show you how to win a couple of dollars for every series while still limiting your losses per series, then this book will be worth 80 times the cost.

In the previous chapter, I showed you the theory behind the D'Alembert. Now I will cover some variations that can be utilized in a series. I am very adamant about you realizing the power of the casinos when they place minimums on a table. The average visitor cannot combat these minimums with their lack of bankroll, knowledge, money management, and discipline.

In this method of betting, I would like you to adopt a partial pattern for your series. I will list several that could be used at the $5 table.

### FIVE DOLLAR TABLE:
a) Aggressive...$5 $10 $15 $20 $25 (Max. $25)
b) Semi Aggressive...$5 $8 $12 $17 $23 (Max. $23)

    c) Normal. . .$5  $7  $10  $14  $19      (Max. $19)
    d) Conservative. . .$5  $7  $9 $11 $13   (Max. $13)
    e) Super Conservative. . .$5  $6  $7  $8  $9  $10
                                    (Max. $10)

Notice that each series started with $5. You decide on one which would appeal to you, or make up your own, and stick to it. If your series is still alive when you reach the maximum bet, which is five numbers, kill the series, take your loss, and start over at another table. Think this will be hard to do? You bet your sweet tooth it will. When you acquire the guts to walk away from a losing table before going broke, you're starting to put your game together. And I did say 'guts'.

If you choose Method A, you could lose $75 during a bad series. This would be 50% of your $150 session money. So wave bye-bye to that table. Your one series destroyed the session, since you played a too aggressive system with short money.

Let's take a less aggressive approach. Try Method E. If you take a bath with that series, your total loss would be only $45. This is with allowing six losses instead of the usual five shown in the other four methods. You could stop this E Method at $9 as your highest bet. That would leave you only $35 as your maximum outlay. Or, you could make your highest bet $8. This would lower your possible maximum loss in a series to $26. With this approach and a $150 session amount, you'd be able to play at least three series.

Work out your own pattern of bets per series and make them coincide with your session money which is one third of your bankroll.

# MONEY MANAGEMENT 13

## Summary On D'Alembert

Finally, let's base our series on the fact that you can find a table that has a $2 or $1 minimum on the outside wagers. In this case, I'm talking to the majority of players, as you high rollers are already writing out super aggressive series.

At these lower minimum tables, you will be able to stretch out your series to compensate for the absence of the high required first bet. For example:

**TWO DOLLAR TABLE** (Minimum)

a) Aggressive...$2 $4 $6 $8 $10 $12   (Max. $12)
b) Semi Aggressive...$2 $3 $5 $8 $12   (Max. $12)
c) Normal...$2   $3   $5   $7   $10       (Max. $10)
d) Conservative...$2 $3 $4 $5 $6 $7   (Max. $7)

Notice the Loss Limit is still set even though you are at smaller minimum tables. Sure, I know the winning amounts will not be high, but will you please accept the theory of minimizing losses and accepting small wins as opposed to your prevous helter skelter approach?

Look at the conservative Method D. Even allowing for a six-bet loss possibility, your total possible maximum loss can only be $27. If you were to use the Martingale System and still lose, you could be out

$126 for the same number of straight losses, which you'd better realize is possible.

At the $1 minimum table, your total possible loss amounts could be lower:

a) Aggressive...

$1   $2   $4   $7   $11   $16        (Max. $16)

b) Conservative...

$1   $2   $3   $4   $5   $6   $7      (Max. $7)

The important thing is to realize the theory:

a) Always play on a 50-50 betting proposition.

b) Be sure to preset your maximum bet.

c) Write on your pad a unit, or dollar amount bet.

d) If lose, increase next bet one (1) unit or pre-determined dollar amount.

e) If lose, write amount of your next bet on pad.

f) If win, cross out winning amount on pad and bet next lowest amount.

g) When all numbers in series are completed by being crossed off, series is over. Start new one by writing starting number (or bet).

h) Stay within the confines of your session money, and never lose more than 50% of session bankroll.

i) If En Prison Rule comes up in middle of your series, treat it just like a tie and do not change your series bet. Leave it ride until decision is reached.

j) If you'd like, come up with your own series line.

# MONEY
## MANAGEMENT 14

## Labouchere System

Here again, we have a system called Labouchere, named after a gentleman who probably invented it on his own or came up with a variation of the D'Alembert, or vice versa. In any event, it is a theory of betting, and is also called the Cancellation System.

The idea behind this system is to start with a group of numbers which signify your bet, and then you cancel out these numbers as you win and add additional numbers if you lose.

Write on a sheet of paper: 1, 2, 3 — which will comprise your series. Playing only the even money bets on a roulette table, such as black/red, odd/even, or high/low in a game that has the En Prison Rule, you are fighting only a 2.70 vig. On the European wheel, which contains only one zero and the En Prison Rule, this is even better. For in that case the house vig is very small.

But you must limit yourself to playing only where you find either one zero or the En Prison Rule. The casinos that do not offer the En Prison Rule benefit and retain a 5.26 edge. This is too great to overcome.

After you set up your series of 1, 2, 3 on your pad, your first bet will be the total of the two end numbers. In this case, four units (1 + 3). If you win, cross off the 1 and 3 from your chart, and only the 2 will remain. Your next bet will be two units. If you win, cross off the 2 on your chart, and the series is complete. Let's say that the two unit bet loses. Write another 2 on your pad, and bet the total of the line, which is now four units (2 + 2). It looks like this:

    1   2   3   2

Suppose you win the four unit bet. Cross off the 2 and 2, and the series is complete. You've won the total of your original line — six units.

Oh, it's great when it wins, but the problem is that the lines can really become enormous. Let's take a look at a probable run which shows a string of losses. You buy in at a table and decide to make this series on the odd/even wager. You pick even.

Start your series with a line of 1, 2, 3 and bet the total of the two end numbers. Your first bet is four units; you lose, and your line now reads:

    1   2   3   4

The next wager is always the total of the two end numbers. In this case, five units (1 + 4). Again you lose, as odd shows on the wheel. You write the loss into your line:

    1   2   3   4   5

The next bet is six (1 + 5), but this time even comes up. You have a winning total of six units. Cross off the 1 and the 5 and bet the total of the two new end numbers, which again is six (2 + 4).

    1   2   3   4   5

Again you lose. Add the total of the losing bet to the line:

    1   2   3   4   5   6

Your next bet is eight units; even shows; you win. The line reads:

1 2 3 4 5 6

Your next bet is seven units $(3 + 4)$; odd shows; you lose:

1 2 3 4 5 6 7

System now calls for a ten unit bet of $3 + 7$, and you win. By crossing off the 7 and the 3, it leaves only the 4. So that is the amount of your next bet:

1 2 3 4 5 6 7

Even shows, giving you a win of four units. Your line is complete and your profit is six units. In that series, even showed four times while odd came up four times. You won 50% of the time and showed a six unit profit.

All well and good. But look at what took place along the way. You were called on to make heavy bets. If you happened to lose that ten unit bet, the next wager would have called for a thirteen unit bet.

The theory behind this system has merit, but it could get out of hand. One way to offset it is by starting with 1 1 1 or even 1 1, which is conservative. Another possibility is 1 1 2 or 1 2 1.

What this method of betting is trying to accomplish is to allow you to win only about 35% to 40% of the time and still show a profit. Because each time you lose you only add one number to the line. Each time you win you deduct two numbers. Logically, you can win approximately a little over one third of the time and show a profit.

But stop right there. The logic is right, and the knowledge is right because you are smart enough to tackle a game which has only a 2.70 vig. But remember what I said way back in the beginning? You must have *all* of the Big Four to win, not just two or even three segments. In this case you need a strong bankroll to offset the possible run of some bad streaks that could jump the line to a point which would call for you to bet quite heavily. You might lack the money, the guts, or both.

Oh, the theory is OK because you should expect to win almost an even amount of wagers on a 50-50 proposition. But don't discount the bankroll. Starting with a smaller starting line is the natural thing to do. We'll try 1 1 1, which should hold your bets down for awhile. Again, you're betting even. The first wager is two (1 + 1). You lose:

         1    1    1    2

Next bet is three (1 + 2). Again odd shows; you lose.

         1    1    1    2    3

Next bet is four (3 + 1). This time you win, so the line reads:

         1    1    1    2    3̶

The bet is three units (1 + 2), but odd shows for a loss.

         1̶    1    1    2    3̶    3

Now you bet four units and lose the spin.

         1̶    1    1    2    3̶    3    4

Bet is five units, even shows; you win.

         1̶    1̶    1    2    3̶    3    4̶

You drop back to a four unit bet and green shows, calling for the En Prison decision. My theory is to surrender half your bet, and add the two units to the line:

~~1~~ ~~1~~ 1 2 ~~3~~ 3 ~~4~~ 2

You then *repeat* the bet that was made. In this case, four. If it loses, add the 4 to the line. Suppose it wins. Merely deduct any combination of four units:

~~1~~ ~~1~~ ~~1~~ 2 ~~3~~ ~~3~~ ~~4~~ 2

Your next bet is four, and you win. The line is complete.

~~1~~ ~~1~~ ~~1~~ ~~2~~ ~~3~~ ~~3~~ ~~4~~ ~~2~~

You end up with a three unit profit, but notice you had to lay out a five unit bet only once. The series produced one green, four losses, four wins, and still showed a profit of three units.

If you were to start with a line of 1 1, it would take a long losing streak to get you to a point of having to lay out large bets. I strongly suggest you start with 1 1 — that is, if this is the money management method you decide to try.

As in the D'Alembert, be sure and preset a maximum limit you will bet. These lines can jump way up in a short time. I warn you that without this Loss Limit, you could get whacked good.

There's nothing wrong with setting a maximum betting limit of ten units on a line that starts 1 1.

Following are suggested maximum bets, based on the aggressive, or conservative style you choose:

| | | | | |
|---|---|---|---|---|
| 1 | 1 | | | 10 units |
| 1 | 1 | 1 | | 10 units |
| 1 | 1 | 2 | | 12 units |
| 1 | 2 | 1 | | 12 units |
| 1 | 2 | 3 | | 18 units |
| 1 | 2 | 3 | 4 | 30 units |
| 2 | 3 | 4 | | 40 units |

If you are that aggressive that your line starts with anything over 1 2 3, you'd better be prepared to lay out some healthy bets. You'd better have the bankroll to start this heavy a line. For example, with the 2 3 4, your session money would have to be at least $500 before you even thought of taking on that line.

Don't forget. I am talking in terms of units, or $5 chips. The money at risk will be substantially reduced if you could play in Vegas at $1 minimum tables for the even money proposition bets.

But in any event, if you decide to try the Labouchere, start with the smallest line available, which is 1 1. You'll have plenty of time to graduate to the higher levels.

# MONEY MANAGEMENT 15

## Variations Of Labouchere

In the previous chapter, I spoke of units. Normally the tables with $5 minimums on the outside bets will scare away people who cannokt lay out these high bets. This will undoubtedly come up in this type of system. Again, be aware of the danger of trying this method with a short bankroll.

Even starting with a line of 1 1, the average player cannot compete. So it is up to him to find a table with a smaller minimum requirement, preferably a $1 table.

If the line gets to a point where it exceeds your loss limit, just cancel it out, take your loss, cash in at that table, and walk. So you suffered a small loss at a particular session. Don't chase that lost money by pouring in fresh green. Go to another table and start again.

In the long run, if you exercise money management and avoid big losses, the constant, consistent small wins will swallow the small losses and the profits will begin to show.

You'll come up with your own run of numbers, but the aggressive player could try an advanced method. This calls for two, three, or even four lines being in operation at the same time. He could conceivably write down the following lines:

```
1   1   1
1   2   1
1   1   2
```

Using this method he has a high amount of units (or dollars),, and as he wins he can cross off any combinations from any of the three lines. He is not restricted to one line at a time. This allows him to keep his bets low for longer periods of time.

I will spin a wheel using a three line method, and start with a conservative string.

```
1   1   1
1   1   2
1   1   1
```

I will use black/red, with my choice being black.

1st bet...$3. Black shows for a win of $3. I can cross off any number, or combinations of numbers, totalling 3. My experience has been to get rid of the bigger numbers as soon as possible. This way you don't get hooked up somewhere down the line with big bets. In this case, I cross off the following:

```
1   1   1
1   1   2
1   1   1
```

2nd Bet...$2.          Lose

```
1   1   1   2
1   1   2
```

3rd Bet...$3.          Lose

```
1   1   1   2
1   1   2   3
1   1   1
```

4th Bet...$4.          Win

```
    1    1    1    2
    1    1    2    3
    1    1    1
5th Bet . . . $3.              Win
    1    1    1    2
    1    1    2    3
    1    1    1
6th Bet . . . $2.              Lose
    1    1    1    2
    1    1    2    3
    1    1    1    2
7th Bet . . . $3.             Lose
    1    1    1    2
    1    1    2    3
    1    1    1    2    3
8th Bet . . . $4.             Win
    1    1    2    3
    1    1    1    2    3
9th Bet . . . $3.             Lose
    1    1    2    3    3
    1    1    1    2    3
10th Bet . . . $5.            Lose
    1    1    2    3    3    5
    1    1    1    2    3
11th Bet . . . $6.            Win
    1    1    2    3    3    5
    1    1    1    2    3
12th Bet . . . $4.           Lose
    1    1    2    3    3    5
    1    1    1    2    3    4
13th Bet . . . $7.           Win
    1    1    2    3    3    5
    1    1    1    2    3    4
```

14th Bet... $3.          Win

~~1~~  ~~1~~  2  ~~3~~  ~~3~~  ~~5~~

~~1~~  1  1  2  ~~3~~  ~~4~~

15th Bet... $2.          Win

~~1~~  ~~1~~  ~~1~~  2  ~~3~~  ~~4~~

The series is complete. In this grouping of three lines, my biggest bet was $7. I won eight times, as opposed to seven losses. My profit was $10. Notice on bet #13, when I won $7. I could have crossed off four numbers (3 2 1 1) and left only the figures 1 and 4. This would have called for only one more win to complete the line, but I did not want to run the risk of losing that five unit bet, and, thereby, start jumping my subsequent bets to higher levels.

On one hand, I would not have to win as many decisions when I cross out three and four numbers with a win, but by eliminating the higher figures, I'm able to keep my bets low.

If you think you'd like to try this method, work out your own line or lines and completely understand the theory before you put it into play with real money.

# MONEY
## MANAGEMENT  **16**

## Summary Of Labouchere

By now I hope you have become aware of a very important facet in gambling. Whichever game you choose, don't be a big shot by strolling up to the table thinking you're Mr. Cool and getting involved in a game in which you are not an expert. I didn't say good. I said expert. You need a purpose and a battle plan after you have knowledge, and that's why I'm laying several methods out in front of you — one or two that you may like to concentrate on.

The Labouchere has its good points and its drawbacks. The good points are naturally a controlled way of playing. You have the opportunity of having to win less decisions than the house, and still come out with a profit.

The drawback, as in most gambling games, is the necessity of having to sometimes make large bets when you reach a dry spell. There is also the possibility that sometimes you will be forced to close out a series at a loss in order to prevent having to make an extra bet and seeing it lose, and having that one extra bet wipe out your remaining session money. When the losses come, learn to take them as part of the game, but don't let them wipe you out. You must learn to limit your losses. Going broke is a NO-NO. As my old pappy used to say, "The chicken who turns and runs away still lives to play another day."

If the Labouchere meets your fancy, here's a few things to remember:

1. Pick a starting line that is in tune with your bankroll. I suggest 1 1 to start.

2. Try to play at the lowest minimum table you can, which allows more fluctuation in your lines.

3. Start by betting the total of the front and back of your line.

4. When you win, cross off the numbers that you bet as a total. For example, if you bet seven units and won, cross off the 2 and 5, 6 and 1, or 3 and 4 — whichever numbers total the winning bet.

5. When you lose, add the number of dollars or units that you lost to your line, and the next bet will be that number, plus the first number in the line.

6. Set a limit as to your maximum bet, either in units or dollars. The chart I gave you previously is a good base to begin with.

7. Set a loss limit on your session money. When you reach it, leave the table.

8. Set a win goal. When you reach it, cut it in half with 50% going into your pocket and the other half staying in play. As you win each succeeding series, continue to put 50% of the profits away and keep 50% with your excess. When the excess goes, so do you.

After you have accumulated some profits from the 1 1 line, start going to 1 1 1 and 1 1 2 if you have the starting bankroll. Eventually, I'd like to see you try the triple line of:

```
1   1   1
1   1   2
1   1   1
```

The fluctuation of betting possibilities will stay low for a long time, due to the many 1s that appear.

# 17 MONEY MANAGEMENT

## Action Numbers

Concentrate on this system. It will lead to a multiple series of plays. This method will place your bets on numbers that are in action all the time. Look at the numbers I will give you and then check to see where they are located on the wheel.

Every roulette wheel is the same, and the numbers are all located in the same position on every wheel in any casino. The numbers, as I explained earlier, are spread in such a way around the wheel so as to separate the continuity and prevent mathematical geniuses from inventing methods of cracking the game.

A great deal of effort was put into separating these numbers; but, naturally, there are a few instances where you can exploit a weakness. I remind you of a certain bet on the layout called the 6 number line, where you receive six numbers with one bet. For instance, you could place a bet between the 1 and 4 overlapping into the first dozen, and you get the numbers 1 - 2 - 3 - 4 - 5 - 6.

I bring your attention to the numbers 10 - 11 - 12 -13 - 14 - 15 - 21, and will refer to them as the action numbers. Look at the wheel and see where these action numbers are positioned. Notice that they are spread around the wheel in such a manner as to be no more than six slots away from each other. In some cases, merely four slots separate two of the numbers. Randomly, drop the ball into one of the slots that does not include one of the action numbers. Notice how close you are to one of the action numbers; hence, the name. They are spread around the wheel in such a way as to be in action all the time. Now, by playing these numbers consistently, it does not mean you *have* to win. But when you do have a bet, you're in action — all the time.

In gambling, minimizing your losses is a major necessity in any endeavor. I stress this fact over and over. When you realize this factor, a tremendous new approach will engulf your game.

That is the theory behind the action numbers. They reduce your chances of losing because you are constantly flirting with the section or slot, where that little ball will land. Also, by playing the action numbers as a group, you can limit the amount of your bets until you start to win. For instance, let's say the minimum at a certain table is $2 inside. You are using 50¢ chips. If you placed a 50¢ chip on each of the six numbers, you would have $3 at risk.

However, by placing the bet in such a way that you get all six numbers in the lines, you only have to put up four chips, or two, or anything you'd like. The vig against you and the payoff percentage are exactly the same, but you are controlling your bankroll until your run comes. If you bet four chips on the action numbers and one of them hits, you will be paid off @

5-1, which would mean a payoff of 20 chips for the four you invested. In that case, I would increase my next bet to five chips, and as I continued to hit one of the action numbers, I would keep increasing my bets until my goal was reached.

We get into theory here, as some people will figure that since a number hit, it is not 'due' to hit again for some time. I approach it in the vein that when it hits, the trend is in my favor, and I would like to ride it out.

Let's go down to the lower part of the layout for another group of action numbers. In this case, it is the six number cluster of two lines: 28 - 29 - 30 - 31 - 32 - 33. Here, again, it requires a bet on the outside section between the 28 and 31 and overlapping into the area of the third dozen. Now you have covered another six numbers on the board.

Examine the wheel to find where this new group of numbers is located. Notice that they are also spread around the wheel in approximately the same places as the first seven. What you have done is increased your chances of winning by reducing the areas between the first seven numbers where that ball may drop. Now you are covering 13 slots on the board; but, more importantly, you have intelligently spread the bets on the layout to cover a controlled section of the wheel.

A note on the number 21, which is included as part of the first set of action numbers: Instead of placing a chip straight up on number 21, you could take the four number cluster of 17, 18, 20 & 21 for that single chip.

Assuming you placed three chips on each of the

two double streets, and one chip on the four number grouping of 17, 18, 20 & 21, you now have sixteen numbers working for you and only 7 chips, or $3.50 at risk.

You can be sure that if you play these two groupings and the dealer spins that ball into play, there will be thirteen strong numbers in action for you.

# 18 MONEY MANAGEMENT

## Betting The Action Numbers

The power of this system is that the 10, 11, 12, 13, 14, 15, 21, 28, 29, 30, 31, 32, and 33 are ideally spaced around the wheel in such a way that you stay in action all the time. Your chances of losing is reduced, due to the small amount of losing possibilities. There are opportunities to use various forms of money management systems, but the main power of this play is the chance to cover sixteen numbers with seven chips.

You are aware of the chance to play, for example, three chips on each of the double streets. With the number 21, you get the chance to use the four number cluster with one chip. The payoff on the double streets is 5-1, while the four number payoff is 8-1.

In this way, the patron with a small bankroll can cover all sixteen numbers with seven 50¢ chips. This is a total of only $3.50 at risk. If a win occurs on one of the three different bets, increase that particular grouping by one unit on the next spin.

You could start the series with five chips on each of the double streets and two chips on the 21 cluster. The amount of variations are unlimited. My suggestion is to increase the winning section by one chip each time it hits.

I'm aware that the 0 - 00 can wipe me out, but in any form of gambling there is always the possibility of loss. If you do lose, don't set there sulking like a whipped cur. Nobody likes to lose, but if you do, take it in stride. Don't act like the world just caved in. Losses will occur. Accept them.

You could use a form of the D'Alembert system by setting a loss limit and win goal with these numbers. It will take a lot of paperwork, and I suggest a table with very low minimums, probably 10¢ or 25¢, and no more. Set the loss limit in advance. The fact that you are playing with small valued chips, with several possibilities, will prevent your having to lay out gigantic sums of money. But, you must base these loss limits on your session money and bankroll. First, take the time to completely understand the D'Alembert system before converting that method to this action number category.

Another method of using the Action Numbers is pre-determining a series of spins. Suppose you set five spins as your maximum session output. You could wager the following number of chips per spin: 7 - 7 - 9 - 11 - 13. This is your total chip outlay. If all five spins lose, that session is over. Based on each chip being worth 50¢, your total outlay, assuming you lose all five spins, would be 47 chips. At 50¢ per chip, you lose only $23.50, a small amount by which to test the table.

If you lost all five spins, that session is over, and you leave the table. But your losses are small and you're able to start a new session without being in a lot of trouble. Based on the fact that these numbers are so well spread around the table, it will be very seldom that you will not get at least one hit in five spins. Let's say you reached the fifth spin, without a hit, and placed five chips on each of the double streets, and three chips on the 21 cluster. You are already out 34 chips, based on the 7 - 7 - 9 - 11 - 13 series. Assume the number eight showed, giving you a victory. You lose eight chips from the other two bets, giving you a deficit of 42 chips. But, you receive a 5-1 payoff, or 25 chips, for hitting the number 8. That reduces your total losses, in five spins, to only seventeen chips, or $8.50, and you had only one single hit in five spins.

The next bet? Put six chips on the double street that hit (where the 8 is located), and put the same five bet outlay on the 28 - 33 double street, and three chips on the 21 cluster.

Again, the variations, or combinations of bets can be made at your own discretion. But, they must be determined ahead of time, in order for you to control your money, and minimize your losses. You only increase your bets as you win.

Take some time right now to set up several series, using the 10 - 15, and the 28 - 33 double streets, and the 21 cluster of four numbers as choices. Your total outlay of chips per spin can be the table minimum, and based on your bankroll. Set a loss limit of spins, and a hard and fast rule for increasing your bet on the numbers that are hitting. Keep your loss limit and win goal in check. If your numbers aren't hitting, then stop. When you get a profit, use my split system. Learn to win and walk.

# MONEY MANAGEMENT 19

## Variations Of Action Numbers

You know, you're not locked into playing only the six line groups. I stress that one simply because it allows you less chance of losing by giving you more numbers on the board. But, you could use this same approach with the three number line or the four number group. I'll go over the four cluster, which pays 8-1, and, naturally, you have any group of four numbers by placing your bet directly in the center of your choice.

### FOUR NUMBER GROUPING

| SPIN NUMBER | AMOUNT OF BET (chips) | IF LOSE TOTAL LOSS (chips) | IF WIN PRO-JECTED PROFIT (chips) |
|:---:|:---:|:---:|:---:|
| 1 | 6 | 6 | 48 |
| 2 | 6 | 12 | 42 |
| 3 | 6 | 18 | 36 |
| 4 | 6 | 24 | 30 |
| 5 | 6 | 30 | 24 |
| 6 | 6 | 36 | 18 |
| 7 | 6 | 42 | 12 |
| 8 | 6 | 48 | 6 |
| 9 | 7 | 55 | 8 |
| 10 | 8 | 63 | 9 |

| 11 | 9  | 72 | 9 |
|----|----|----|---|
| 12 | 10 | 80 | 8 |

That's a long enough series. You want to go higher — go ahead if you've got the bankroll. But for those with short bankrolls, this gives you twelve spins and playing the 50¢ chips, your maximum loss is $40. If you decide to go for less spins, good, do it. Maybe eight spins could be your limit with a maximum loss total of 48 units or $24, with the use of 50¢ chips.

The four number groupings you should use, based on the same theory as the six number streets, are also spread around the wheel in a pretty good mix. These are a few:

a) 5, 6, 8, 9
b) 10, 11, 13, 14
c) 19, 20, 22, 23

Play all three groupings at the same time. The spread on the wheel gives you an excellent variety of sections.

Finally, you could work the same method with the three number lines using the same basic approach. In this case, the three number line pays 11-1.

**THREE NUMBER LINES:**

| SPIN NUMBER | AMOUNT OF BET (chips) | IF LOSE, TOTAL LOSS (chips) | IF WIN, PRO-JECTED PROFIT (chips) |
|---|---|---|---|
| 1 | 6 | 6  | 66 |
| 2 | 6 | 12 | 60 |
| 3 | 6 | 18 | 54 |
| 4 | 6 | 24 | 48 |
| 5 | 6 | 30 | 42 |
| 6 | 6 | 36 | 36 |

| 7  | 6 | 42 | 30 |
|----|---|----|----|
| 8  | 6 | 48 | 24 |
| 9  | 6 | 54 | 18 |
| 10 | 6 | 60 | 12 |
| 11 | 6 | 66 | 6  |
| 12 | 7 | 72 | 11 |
| 13 | 8 | 80 | 16 |

Your profits are higher, but you've got less chance of hitting because you have only three numbers. Here again you could take sections of the action numbers. For instance, 10 - 11 - 12 - 28 - 29 - 30, and split your bet money into covering both lines. The payoffs will be lower, as each time you win, you'll receive the 11-1 on the line that hits minus the bet on the other line which didn't. The tables I have given you are based on one three number line, but this can be adjusted to cover any additional lines at the same time.

# 20 MONEY MANAGEMENT

## Summary On Action Numbers

Like any system, this one will work when the trend is in your favor, and won't work when your numbers are cold. But, systems are needed to give you control over your play and help you minimize your losses. The variation on this grouping alone could fill two books. You should perfect the theory of this method and then work out your own method of variations. The basic rules are the same:

1) Never double up to recoup past losses, but bet within the payoff figures that allow the return to cover the previous bets.
2) Pre-determine an intelligent number of bets in a series before stopping.
3) Don't allow your stubborness or gut feelings to influence your keeping a series alive. Don't try to outguess the wheel by thinking that certain numbers or colors are 'due'.
4) Don't be afraid to allow a short number of spins to comprise a series.
5) *Don't* exceed session loss limits. This is the biggest mistake of gamblers and will continue to be the biggest downfall.

The overall approach to a session with a controlled method of play will keep you in the game a long while. Since these numbers I've shown you are positioned in such a way around the table so as to keep you in the game consistently, there is no reason why you won't hit 4 - 5 - 6 numbers in a row. Of course, the returns won't be colossal, as I believe in covering more numbers in an attempt to cut down losses.

But, you will have more consistent wins. Let's see if you don't start to get accustomed to the great feeling that comes with profits.

# 21 MONEY MANAGEMENT

## Multi-Numbered Play

By now you know how much I think about certain parts of gambling, including the all important facet of minimizing your losses. I believe this is the biggest drawback that people who gamble have. It is one of the things that contribute to people getting whacked at gambling. Their small bankrolls don't last long enough to keep them in the games. They bet too heavy, and can't sustain the losses which surely will come.

I try to get across the fact that it is more important to take these smaller wins and, thus, be able to compete longer. The systems I've shown you are given with the intent of having you manage your money in such a way so as to stay alive until you get enough of a profit to allow you to call it a day.

In this multi-numbered system, it emphasizes the fact that the wins will be small but that the losses also are reduced to only a few numbers on the wheel. The system leaves very little margin for loss, since it covers so many numbers. If you'd examine your wheel, you'll find that the numbers you leave open for loss potential are surrounded by numbers that you are covering. In only one instance on the layout will you have two numbers next to each other that give you a large loss. Those two are the 4 and the 16. In all other cases, a losing number will be surrounded by a win or a push.

I would like you, naturally, to play at the lowest minimum inside table you can find. Las Vegas, of course, would provide the ideal situation. In Atlantic City you will probably have to play the $3 inside minimum with 50¢ chips. If you are allowed to use 25¢ chips, do it. You will need twelve of them to hit your minimum, but that is no problem.

I'll assume you're at a $3 minimum table with 50¢ chips. This is much like the hit-and-run system at craps where you go to a table, make a quick hit, and leave. If it embarrasses you to do this, you've got some problem. How anyone can be embarrassed by what a stranger thinks of them while they are trying to win money, completely escapes me.

Since one or two losses at this system will result in a fifteen chip loss, I insist you make your hit and run. The layout is covered by these bets:

a) 2 Chips on the    0 - 00 - 1 - 2 - 3     grouping
b) 2 Chips on the    5 - 6 - 8 - 9     grouping
c) 2 Chips on the    17 - 18 - 20 - 21     grouping
d) 2 Chips on the    22 - 23 - 24     street
e) 4 Chips on the    10 - 11 - 12 - 13 - 14 - 15
     Double Street
f) 4 Chips on the    28 - 29 - 30 - 31 - 32 - 33
     Double Street

Again, this isn't written in stone, but you are looking for a hit on one of the 12 action numbers while covering yourself on sixteen other numbers with various sized bets.

You already know the payoffs for the different bets, but this is what will happen:

If a) shows,  your Net is:  Minus 2 Chips

If b) shows,  your Net is:  Plus 2 Chips

If c) shows,  your Net is:  Plus 2 Chips

If d) shows,  your Net is:  Plus 8 Chips

If e) shows,  your Net is:  Plus 8 Chips

If f) shows,  your Net is:  Plus 8 Chips

In this case, you have 23 numbers that will give you a win. Five will show a mere minus two chips and ten numbers which will take sixteen chips away. Those ten losing numbers are 4 - 7 - 16 - 19 - 25 - 26 - 27 - 34 - 35 - and 36. And, of course, I've already explained that these losing numbers are surrounded by non-losers, which means that you're in action all the time.

In the money management of this method, I advise you to increase each bet by one chip anytime you get a win on either D, E, or F. If that subsequent spin loses, revert back to the basic play.

As you get deeper into the game of roulette, you'll see the multitude of variations of which I speak. For this method, a large bankroll on a table allowing 25¢ chips gives you a tremendous amount of variations. You can start increasing your bets on a winning streak to take advantage of a hot roll, yet allowing you a wide coverage of the other numbers with a minimal outlay of money.

The multitude of variations and betting regressions and progressions would fill about nine chapters. I'd like to take a moment here to give a plug for my casino gambling school, which teaches people how to play and how to win. Knowing how to play is not enough.

When I have a class on roulette, the number of systems and spin-offs of each separate system could go on and on. After a while, the student gets a tremendous grasp of the game and its systems, and can then set up his own betting strategy. It's a genuine pleasure to see these players put the money management and discipline techniques to work.

However, once you pick two or three systems to concentrate on, it is important that you master those few systems and stick with them through at least two sessions. Don't jump back and forth in a session trying various systems.

# 22 MONEY MANAGEMENT

## Wrapping Up Systems

I could go on and on and on and on about various systems to use at the roulette table. That's because with 38 numbers, high/lows, dozens, colors, and combinations of every type, there are many possibilities for different forms of betting and a dozen systems for covering every category.

As I said in the beginning of this section, people have been attacking the tables with every form of system imaginable. This is especially true in the European casinos where the game holds so much intrigue for its patrons. You want to know something? You read about some of these approaches, and it captures your fancy. You try it out at home, and it can't miss. You can't wait to get to the casino to try it for real.

Well, a lot of these systems do work. But after awhile, the player gets bored because he wants to win more money and the grind starts to get to him. He loses control, throws money management out the door and signs his own death warrant. The losing starts and then begins to spiral as the player loses complete control of both his money management and system and starts to try and outguess the wheel.

There is nothing wrong with systems. In fact, I

believe that anyone playing roulette must have a pre-conceived method of play. Get away from that jerky approach of making bets all over the board with no specific plan in mind.

I don't know if I'm getting across to you, but gambling is a serious business. Most people's lacka-daisical approach to it proves what jerks they really are. But just playing system after system after system can be harmful if you start jumping all over the place and not giving the one system that you started with enough time to begin producing. Don't forget you have your loss limits that will always prevent a disaster in any one session.

Most all of the systems will work for a while, but so many people get itchy pants when things don't go their way right off the bat. They don't realize they must wait for the trends to point in their direction and then grab the profits.

I've given you a handful of systems and I'd like you to take a hard look at them and maybe add your own icing on the cake.

- a) Regression System    (Outside Wagers)
- b) D'Alembert System
- c) Labouchere System
- d) Action Numbers
- e) Multi-Numbered System

All five of them have strong points, which, in my humble opinion, outweigh the bad side. For the inside bets, I lean towards the action numbers system. For the outside, I naturally lean towards my own regression system.

Now don't go getting impatient, if you try one of these systems and the money doesn't start rolling in. They are designed to help you manage your money. It is only one fourth of the Big Four, but so important. In the case of roulette, the systems act on actually two cylinders covering both knowledge and money management.

Pick one of these. Study it, perfect it, and try it. I think you'll be pleasantly surprised.

# MONEY MANAGEMENT 23

## You And Money Management

In these chapters on money management, I've gone over systems that allow you to stay in the game. Get away from your haphazard approach to gambling or get away from gambling altogether. These systems are not locks on getting you to win 96% of the time, but they offer you an intelligent approach to the game of roulette and an awareness of controlling your money.

Next time you're at a casino, take a look at the various individuals at a roulette table just dropping bets all over the layout in a clumsy, uncontrolled, no method, illogical, mish-mash mode of betting. They have no game plan, no idea as to how much they will wager on the spin after a win, or the spin after a loss. They're out of control, and will probably lose. They have no system of play; no money management. Every single bet you make should be pre-determined, based on the previous win or loss, and also the pre-determined amount you will bet, based on that decision.

As I write this page, it is a hot, humid, scorching summer night in August. I have just left the casinos in Atlantic City where I played two sessions of baccarat and one at roulette.

I won $130 at baccarat in my first session, and lost $70 at my second. I then changed games and played roulette. Using the LaBouchere System, I got ahead about $150, lost back $40, and wrapped up the session with a $110 profit. For the day, I showed a $170 win, which is no big deal, but a tough grinding profit spread over approximately four hours.

I am now in a hotel room, writing a few pages of this book about money management. It brings to mind a lecture I gave in North Jersey a few nights ago. There were about 200 people present, and I was discussing casino games.

Suddenly, some guy stands up and loudly proclaims that money management is a lot of crap. He goes to the casinos twice a month with $100. He always loses, but has a good time. He enjoys himself, and doesn't mind the $100 loss since he feels it's worth the money for all the action he gets.

In my humble opinion, that guy is a jerk. Anybody who doesn't mind losing money and then laughs about it, has to be operating with half a deck. I told this guy he was a jerk, and, naturally, that almost created a riot. When order was restored, we got into intelligently discussing the illogical idea of taking money to a casino and pre-determining that you will lose. Not everybody loses in gambling. The casinos offer you the chance to beat them, in a beautiful, comfortable environment. If you're equipped with the Big Four, you have a good chance of taking some of their money. They'll try to overwhelm you with hype, but it's up to you to concentrate on winning. When you get ahead, get moving.

There are scores of people like the man mentioned above. They believe they're supposed to lose. Ridiculous!!! The reason they have lost for so many previous years is due to a lack of money management. Think about your own approach to gambling and money management.

Before I left the lecture hall that night, my adversary tracked me down, apologized for his actions, bought my book on blackjack, and signed up for the card counting course at my school. We talked for over an hour, and he admitted that he accepted his $100 losses because he honestly thought it was impossible to win. After he completes his course, his awareness of money management will change his entire game.

Same goes for any of you who refuse to accept this restrictive method of play. Money management? It is restrictive, and it is hard. But you know something? If each one of you, as an individual, will force yourself to at least try to control your game, for a three-month period, the results will astound you. Will you be a big winner? I don't know!!!

But it will limit your losses. I guarantee it.

# 1    DISCIPLINE

## Discipline — What Is It?

Without the Big Four, you haven't got a chance in gambling. But, of all the facets of the Big Four, none is more important that discipline — absolutely nothing.

Discipline is control. If you have control of yourself in anything, you are in charge. If you're not in control, it results in a helter-skelter approach to whatever you are attempting to do.

Gambling is an art. It is a way of life to thousands of people and an outlet for millions of others. How many people do you see every day rushing to buy a lottery ticket right after breakfast, then, a quick hop to an offtrack betting parlor during lunch break. They interrupt their dinner meal to call their local bookie for a bet on a night baseball game, and then hop in the car for a hectic session of bingo. In the meantime, they plan for a weekend trip to the casinos for a few days of gambling.

You think this is an isolated case??? Think again, my friend. This is a typical day in the lives of many non-professional gamblers. Millions of people gamble every day. But they don't know how. They gamble for the thrill of the action and the excitement, but lack the big ingredient — the ability to win. I hope you have memorized the Big Four and the Little Three. They contain your formula for success.

But mostly they all lead to discipline, and the all important, ultimate goal, winning. To win you must have this discipline. It is the ability to control your play and to set an amount of money you would like to win — based on your starting bankroll. When you reach that win goal, have the discipline and self control to leave that table a winner.

It takes a long, long time to acquire discipline, and then you must keep practicing it. The temptation is always there — to go for the big wins. When you have reached your predetermined win goal, have the discipline and intelligence to quit a winner.

# 2  DISCIPLINE

## Discipline — Who Needs It?

Who needs discipline? Everybody who gambles. Who has discipline? Practically nobody who gambles. Most people I talk to admit they don't have it but realize that unless they acquire it, their chances of winning are miniscule.

Let me be very blunt at this point. If you are not going to absorb everything I say in the next few chapters, you may as well send your money to the casinos now. Discipline is the single most important part of the Big Four. You won't agree with the restrictive conditions I will give you, but, if I can reach just a small percentage of people, then the section on discipline is a huge success.

Discipline is not only restricted to crap shooters and blackjack players. It pertains to roulette, slot, and baccarat players as well. And it doesn't stop there. Discipline must be adhered to by the sports bettors, horse players, all the way over to the Bingo players, and the daily lottery hopefuls. There are discipline rules for the poker and gin rummy loyalist as well.

I've covered the money management and discipline systems for the slot players. The bingo and lottery people would do well to adhere to what I'm saying. I have published money management and discipline systems on bingo, lottery, sports, etc. Believe me, getting those people to try it was rougher than getting Sophia Loren's personal phone number.

You couldn't believe the happy feeling of accomplishment that they had when they wrote me of the change in their approach to these daily and weekly gambling habits.

Let me lay it right on the line, my friend. YOU need discipline, and when you get it, your entire gambling approach will improve.

# 3    DISCIPLINE

## The Author — And Discipline

If you ever wanted to find someone with no discipline, you'd need to look no farther than the author. I was the king-sized jerk of all time. Man, when I first started gambling, I couldn't even spell the word discipline. Every casino I entered, I pictured myself owning it by the end of the day. Since I knew so much about gambling, I just naturally felt that it was impossible for me to lose.

The more I learned about every facet of gambling, the more amazed I became that my pockets were not lined with gold. How was it possible that a person could be so smart, and yet always so broke. Well, both ends of that sentence is true. I knew all there was to know about every game available to bet on. My knowledge level was at full, but my wallet was always on E. Something was wrong, but I was too stupid to realize what it was.

There were days when I doubled, tripled, and even quintupled my starting bankroll and was still sitting there trying to win the east wing of the casino. I don't have to go into the gory details of how or why, but the bottom line was that I always gave it back. And I then compounded the stupidity by reaching into my pocket and losing my bankroll, trying to get back the money I had previously won and given back. A vicious cycle?? You bet your life it was.

I can remember the many, many, many nights in Las Vegas when I would play maybe forty straight hours of poker, blackjack, or craps and still leave the game broke. I didn't say I left the game down a few dollars. I said dead broke; not a dime left in my pockets. Then I'd play my silly game of eating a good hearty dinner. When I got to the cashier, I'd go through the act of looking for my money—which I knew was gone.

Most of the time the manager would wave an OK because I had the good sense to leave some healthy tips when I had money. But there still were the times when I had to work off the meal.

You've probably heard the stories about the guy who had to wash dishes because he didn't have the bread to pay for his meal. Let me tell you right now what 'washing the dishes' was comprised of. The first time I had to 'pay for my meal', I figured I'd have to spend about 15-20 minutes doing a load of plates.

My 'drill sergeant' took me to a sink that was loaded with plates that must have been backed up for six days. First, I had to scrape, rinse, scrub, and dry at least 4000 items consisting of cups, plates, silverware, and glasses. When I was done, I was led to a slop sink containing about 40 pots and pans that had to be shined before they passed inspection. Then came two more loads of dishes, a complete mopping of the kit-chen, and, overall, a solid six or seven hours of cons-tant KP duty.

All the while, I'm thinking of all the money I had

in my hands only ten or twelve hours sooner. Sometimes, I'd be betting $400 or $500 on a single hand of poker, and now I was slaving for a meal.

Reality was a long time coming, and it didn't come to me overnight. I spent many, many years chasing the rainbow — looking for the big kill. But, think about it. What is the big kill? To some players, $1000 is a pot of gold. To others, $5000 would just about satisfy them. And then there are some who wouldn't be content with $10,000.

The lottery player who risks 50¢ is mad because he receives only $74 as his return on a winning number. He gets 168 times his return on his investment, and he's still griping. He doesn't know how to win. Surely, you've even had these feelings yourself.

Self-analysis takes a long time to grab you. I know it did with me. I wish I had even 10% of all of the money I gave back after I was ahead in a gambling casino.

When the reality of what I was doing finally hit me, my entire game changed. Discipline was the answer — it was the key. I adhere to a strict brand of disciplined play and I preach this method to every person who attends my school or lectures. And I say it to you right now: "Don't be a dummy — like this dummy was — Learn How To Win..."

# DISCIPLINE 4

## How Much Should I Win??

This is the question that most people want to have the answer to. And this is the answer they least like to hear — 10%!!! Now, before you punch your bride in frustration, try and see the logic of this statement. Most of you have a bank account where you have stashed away a couple of dollars to buy that second home or cover a college education or to just pad your retirement nest egg.

You leave this money in the bank for a whole year to pick up a paltry 5% return, and pat yourself on the back for being a financial wizard. Yet, you'll go to a casino with a $200 bankroll, a shaky knowledge of the game you're playing, no money management at all, and a complete lack of discipline. You're missing all of the facets of the Big Four. You have set a goal of $1500 for the day starting with $200. Doesn't that sound typical and ridiculous? Of course it does. You're playing a game that, at best, gives you a 50-50 chance of winning and you want over a 700% return on your money — in one day. Even though you accept 5% over a full year for your savings, I fail to see the logic of this. And don't go telling me that you only go to the casinos for a good time or to just have a little fun. It's a ridiculous, silly, expensive way to have fun.

I didn't restrict you to 10%, I merely set your win goal at a realistic figure. Let's take it step by step.

You go into a casino with a certain amount of money. It is called your bankroll. We'll make it $600. This is the money you expect to put at risk. Since gambling runs in streaks, or trends, you don't want to risk a great deal of money at a table where the trend may be going against you. So, you try to avoid getting caught at a cold table. This is done by splitting your bankroll into thirds. In this way, you have eliminated the possibility of getting whacked in one single game.

When you split the bankroll into thirds, each third then becomes a session. You will go to the first table with $200 or one third of your bankroll. You will play at that first roulette table until you lose $100, or 50% of the $200 session money, which will be your loss limit. You don't have to lose the whole 50%. It is up to each person to decide what his or her own personal loss limit per session will be. You can set 50%, 40%, 30%, 25%, anything that makes you feel comfortable. But no more than 50%. That's discipline.

Go to the other side of the coin. With the $200 session money, you will play until you win 20%, or $40. Think about it for three or four seconds. You are playing a game of roulette which has either a 5.26% or 2.70% vig against you, depending on which part of the layout your bets are placed. And, you get ahead 20%. That's an accomplishment.

The next step calls for you to split that $40 profit in half, putting half of it, or $20, in your pocket, along with your $200 starting session money. That $20 profit can never be touched again at this session. In reality, it is a profit of 10%, which is what I want you to learn to accept. But, remember, you still have the other half of your winnings, or $20, to keep in play. This is called excess. As long as this excess money remains on the table, you will stay at that session. When it is gone, your session is over, and you leave that table.

The third and last part of the procedure is called a series. Bankroll is number one, and it is divided into sessions. When you place your first bet at a session, it is called a series. As long as you keep winning, that series stays alive. When a loss occurs, that series is over and you begin another one.

OK, you've won $40, cut it in half, pocketed $20, and left $20 in play. The next series starts with $7 spread around the layout. You catch a few good spins, and run your series money up to a $16 profit before a loss occurs. Split the $16 in half. Eight dollars goes in your pocket, and $8 stays in play with your excess.

As you keep having winning series, you keep splitting those wins in half and depositing 50% in with your guaranteed take, leaving 50% with the excess. What you are doing is increasing the amount of money you are guaranteed to take from that table, and increasing the excess money you have to play with.

When the trend turns against you and you start to lose that excess money, grab a few chips and kill that session. You don't have to play down to your final chip in the excess pile.

As you become more and more proficient at gambling, you can slowly increase your win goal to 25% and maybe even 30% before calling for a split. But, until you do become proficient, start with 20%

and then the split will give you a 10% guaranteed profit.

The loss limit I leave to you. If you'd like to set a 33% loss limit, great. You don't have to go all the way to the 50% level. The biggest thing is forcing yourself to set these limits and then follow them.

You think this is going to be hard to do??? You can bet your mother-in-law, it'll be hard. It will seem fruitless and mostly like a waste of time. But it's a start. The people who'll cry the most about it are the ones who go to a casino with $200 and are asked to look for a 10%, or $20 win profit. Well, how much did you logically expect to win with a lousy $200??? You want to win more? Bring more.

For now, Learn How To Win. Or, have I said that to you before?

# DISCIPLINE  5

## The Professional Gambler

Just for kicks, write down what you think a professional gambler is like. I'll bet the description doesn't rival the way you picture Santa Claus or the Easter Bunny. Naturally, it shouldn't. But, it also shouldn't compare with your description of Satan himself.

A professional gambler just doesn't like to work. In my case, I detest anything that requires effort for its accomplishment. But I do have discipline — as do all professional gamblers. Actually, that is the only thing that separates the novice from the pro. Everything else should be equal; namely, bankroll, knowledge (which the novice could acquire), and money management.

I'll bet your description or idea of what that type of person is like did not include a reference to discipline, control, or conservative behavior. And actually, these attributes pertain to the professional who makes his living at gambling. He wouldn't think of making bets — just to compete — just to stay in the game. Every bet is made with a definite purpose in mind based on the best percentage move for that particular game.

The temptation to take a real shot on a given day is always there, but with the logical realization that if he loses his bankroll on that day, it's quite possible he's going to have to go out and get a job. That scary proposition alone keeps plenty of pros in line.

But the point is — if the pro practices discipline, why shouldn't the novice? Another curious thing is the approach to gambling that separates the pro and the novice. The pro tries to learn every single thing he can about a certain game, while the novice will take a scant amount of knowledge about that same game and risk his money at it.

I explained in a previous chapter about the typical day in the life of a novice who dabbles on the lotteries, horses, ball games, and bingo in a single day and throws in a little poker game on the side. The pro usually sticks with one or two games and concentrates on just that one area.

I know of some horse players who have never entered a casino and have no desire to do so. In the same vein, some people who are expert card counters have never been able to determine a horse's head from his elbow. Ever try to get a crap shooter to get interested in a poker game? He'd fall asleep after four hands. Some of the sharpest gin rummy players I know would take three days to decide if Willie Mays played quarterback for the Jets, center for the Lakers, pitched for the Yankees, or was Billie Jean King's doubles partner at Wimbledon. And yet they are professional gamblers at gin rummy.

You'd be amazed at how many pros concentrate on just one outlet. That's because they want to be sure they are perfect at the game where they will be risking their money. Now that makes sense. Why shouldn't you be perfect at anything where you risk your money?

Then how can the novice be so naive as to bet on

anything he sees without even being good at these games? The pro realizes the importance of the Big Four and the novice disdains it. Guess who loses more often . . .

# 6 DISCIPLINE

## The Big Shot

How this dope amuses me! You'll find this clod at every racetrack, in every casino, and involved in almost every betting venture. He's the Big Shot — the big mouth — the big spender — the plunger — the jerk. He's all of this and more.

I will never be able to understand these guys who lose $1000 on a given day, and then have the audacity to laugh and joke about it, and act like it doesn't even matter. This jerk wouldn't pick up the tab for two cups of coffee. He carries pennies in his pocket to make sure he doesn't tip the waitress more than exactly 15%.

His kids get hand-me-down bicycles from third cousins, and he bets black $100 chips on the roulette table. When he loses, he throws $10 to the dealers as a gesture of being a big shot, and then rushes home to brag about his losses.

Being a big bettor does not make you a good bettor. I, personally, never go to anything higher than a $5 table at blackjack or craps. Why should I? You can bet higher amounts at a $5 table, but the important thing is to bet smaller amounts until you get on a winning trend. The Big Shot isn't happy unless he's making bets high enough to shrink his socks when he loses. But he has this silly image that he thinks he has to play up to.

Don't be a Big Shot. Play within your bankroll and within your session money. Play smart.

# DISCIPLINE 7

## Your Own Personal Goal

Well, I've had my say on what I think should be your Loss Limit and your Win Goal. Following is the breakdown pertaining to each game offered in the casino:

| GAME | WIN GOAL | LOSS LIMIT |
|------|----------|------------|
| Craps | 25% | 50% |
| Blackjack | 20% | 40% |
| Baccarat | 30% | 60% |
| Roulette | 25% | 50% |
| Slots | (See section regarding Systems) | |
| Big Wheel | a No-No | |
| Keno | 20% | 40% |
| Poker | 40% | 60% |

You can set your own goals, but not when you get to the table. Set them beforehand, like right now. And stick to the percentages you decide upon. You're not going to win all the time. That's impossible. But when you do lose, these losses will be minimized. When you win, the method I showed you on controlling your sessions will result in more consistent, small wins, thus keeping your bankroll alive and allowing you to be able to compete in a more controlled fashion.

First you decide on your bankroll. Whatever you decide upon, it's impossible to go broke because of the

Loss Limit that will always restrict the amount you can lose. Next, you must become perfect at the game you choose. If it's roulette, pick one of the systems, perfect it, and then lay out your betting methods. Decide on what amount you will set as your loss limit, and another hard-core decision on what your win goal will be. Then stick to it. Set your limits now so that you learn to be disciplined. Get into the habit of letting a strict method of control dictate your gambling.

Don't worry. Little by little you can raise those figures. But to get your feet wet, start slow.

# DISCIPLINE 8

## Learn How To Win

Look at the front cover of this book and, in fact, every book I've written, or will write. In the upper right hand corner are the words: "Learn How To Win". I have referred to these words on several occasions in this book and I want you to dwell on them for just a moment.

It doesn't say Learn How to Play. It says: "Learn How to Win". Winning is the name of the game, regardless of how many people try to appease themselves by saying that they play for enjoyment rather than playing to win. The truth is, they don't know how to win.

That great football coach, Vince Lombardi, laid it right on the table when he said, "Winning is not the most important thing — it's the only thing". No beating around the bush by Lombardi. No trying to spread out the garbage that it doesn't matter if you win or lose, but just that you had a good time. Hogwash! He goes right to the heart of the matter. Win—or else you have nothing.

I've heard some other cute little sayings, one of which stands out in my mind. "It isn't important if you win or lose — it's how you play the game". Of all the blankety blank nonsense. That one has to be placed near the top of hypocritical sayings. I'm a card counter in blackjack, and play an excellent game. I consider myself a class poker player, and I also pitch 'fast pitch' softball four nights a week. Let me tell you, when I leave that blackjack table or poker session or walk off that softball field a loser, I am sick. Believe me, I'm not a sore loser. I congratulate the opposing team or the other poker players. And I never show emotion by slamming down my cards, kicking the wall, or shouting out a stream of curses.

I hate to lose, and do not find comfort in the fact that I "played a good game". Examine your own reaction when you lose. You could lose a tennis match 6-7, 6-4, 6-7, and feel downright rotten, even though it's obvious you played three good sets.

Acquire the ability and desire to win and work at it. If you lose, take it with an outward display of class, despite the fact your guts are tearing up inside. I want you to want to win and not just gamble for fun. If you don't think you are capable of winning at gambling, then stop right now.

And laugh in the face of the next hypocrite who looks at you and says, "It's not important that you won or lost — look at the great time we had."

Set your sights on winning. Be it 30%, 25%, 20%, 10%, or 5%.. Learn How To Win.

# DISCIPLINE 9

## Wrapping Up Discipline

I think you've got the idea of what discipline is, so I'll merely list the steps to follow:

1.  Set aside an amount of money which you will gamble with on a given day.
2.  Set your loss limit before you enter the casino.
3.  Set your win goal before you enter the casino.
4.  In roulettte, 50% is a decent Loss Limit.
5.  In Slots, set aside only a percentage of your overall bankroll and play either the Straight 60 or the Chicken Approach Method, or build your own mousetrap.
6.  Divide your bankroll into three sessions.
7.  After you win the set percentage of your session, cut it in half and guarantee a win for that session. Subsequent series wins should be then divided in half with 50% placed with your guarantee and 50% added to your excess.
8.  If you play my regression 2 - 1 - 2 system, always make the first bet of a series higher than the table minimum so that you can regress back down.

9.  Leave the table if you lose the first five spins.
10. Never play at a table unless you have at least 30 times the amount of the minimum (40 times is the desired amount).
11. Learn to divide your profit when you win the pre-determined amount that you set. This will be hard.
12. Learn to walk when you lose the pre-determined Loss Limit. This will also be hard to do.
13. Finally — learn discipline.

If you can force yourself to adhere to these few rules, you will be on the way to becoming a strong player. Discipline is tough to acquire and hard to maintain. But since it guarantees results, it is well worth the effort.

Listen to what Webster's dictionary says about discipline: ". . . Chastisement by way of correction and training: hence, training through *suffering*".

Yeah, you'll suffer a little, but the fruits of victory taste very sweet. Grab yourself a mouthful.

# ODDS & ENDS

# 1

## Entering A Casino

It's a good idea to know how to handle yourself in a casino. Remember, you're a guest there. Being a loud mouth, a Big Shot, or a crybaby will only antagonize the casino personnel, who can spot a greenhorn immediately. On the other hand, they will just as quickly cater to the class individual who knows how to conduct himself.

When you enter a casino, you don't have to race up to the first table you see to begin playing. Whatever game you decide to play, get in the habit of charting a table. Watch the flow of the game to see if the trend at that table is in the direction that you will be playing. For instance, if you're going to concentrate on the color black, wait for ten spins to see what the pattern is. Suppose red shows seven times, and black three. Don't go thinking that black is 'due'. Merely move to another table and start charting all over again.

When you pick a table, merely place your buy-in session money on the layout in front of you. The dealer will take the money, count it, and give you an amount of chips to coincide with your money. If you want to break down your chips to the least value of chips at that table, just place the higher valued chip ($5 chip) in front of you and say, "Change please". The dealer will take the $5 chip and exchange it for five $1 chips.

If you fall into a losing streak, calmly return your chips to the dealer at the roulette table and tell her to "Cash me in, please". The dealer will change the colored roulette chips for a like amount of money in regular casino chips ($5 or $1 chips).

If you want to buy-in to a game, you buy your chips at the table where you will be playing. In roulette, you will be given a certain color of chips that only you can use at that table until you turn that color back in and leave that table. Do not leave the roulette table with that particular table's chips, as they are of no value at any other table.

When you are finished for the day, bring your chips to the cashier where they will be turned into cash.

One final note. Suppose you have only about $12 in chips left, which shouldn't happen if you follow my money management method. Don't be a jerk by thinking it is only a few dollars, and decide to "give them away" at some game because you're to embarrassed to turn in only a few chips.

It's money, my friend. And I've seen people go up to a table and practically throw away several dollars to avoid going to the cashier with this small amount. What a shame. . .

# ODDS AND ENDS

## Cheating Dealer In Roulette

This one really gets me. It has to do with the cheating dealer who, to begin the next game has to pick up the ball and spin it around the upper lip of the wheel. The story goes that this cheating dealer will wait until a certain section of the wheel will come his way and will spin the ball at that precise second and at the exact speed as he did on the previous spin, to get the ball to drop into the same section as the prior call. Got it?

What a joke. How can anyone possibly believe this nonsense? And worse, how can someone actually put money at risk with this myth? Take a look at the roulette wheel. That ball is going to have to spin several times around the top of the wheel and then when it finally drops into the pit of the wheel, has to contend with approximately six protruding attachments on the wall of the wheel which will cause the ball to jump and hop all over the place.

And finally, each slot is separated by sections which further cause that ball to keep skipping around. I don't care if your husband is working the wheel. Nobody short of the divine Lord can be that perfect to offset that slew of obstacles and get a little white ball to fall into a certain section.

This is another case of where people have heard that the dealer can control where the ball will fall by spinning it at the same speed from the same spot each game.

Another case of people coming up with a ridiculous theory that they can outguess and outthink a mechanical game of chance.

# ODDS AND ENDS   3

## Tipping

Tipping is a touchy subject, and one that can only be based on logic and opinion. Do you tip the dealers? Can they help you? I'll speak from my own personal experiences. First of all, dealers are human beings that deal (no pun intended) with people all day. They talk personally with them and spend hours with this person only a few inches away from them. Suppose I placed a bet on the table for this particular dealer. This is done by putting a chip, either $1, $2, $5, or whatever amount you desire, next to your normal bet. That signifies that this extra bet will be for the dealer. If you win your bet, he wins. If you lose, he suffers the same fate. Only difference is that it doesn't cost the dealer any money.

If the hand wins and I had placed a $1 chip for the dealer, he would place a $1 chip next to the bet, take both the chips, tap the table to alert the pit boss of what is happening, and drop the $2 into the box that is there to hold the dealer's tips. They are split among all of the dealers on that shift. In Las Vegas each dealer gets to keep his own chips.

But now you have put this dealer into a position of wanting to 'repay' the person who 'duked' him. He will make sure that you don't make any sloppy mistakes with your future play. He will watch to make sure your wins are properly paid off and that a cocktail waitress is on ready call.

And also, he may occasionally slip into lapses of forgetfulness. Since the dealer is human, he will sometimes forget to take your bet when you lose, or will accidentally pay you when you actually lose a hand.

I, personally, have found some dealers to become quite lapse after they receive a couple of tips. And why not? These dealers work hard and actually deserve to be tipped. Then, again, if the player does get reciprocated from a dealer on a certain losing play, he tends to return to the casino where the slip happened. This helps the bosses of that casino.

The pit boss has been known to look the other way when a dealer falls into a charitable period. But don't forget, that pit boss was once a dealer and realizes that certain things have a way of happening.

I don't think it's a bad idea to tip the dealer. The best time is after you get ahead. Play a hand for him and then every five or six hands continue to test the water, so to speak.

If you find that this dealer suddenly falls prey to some generous mistakes in your favor, continue to tip. If he doesn't acknowledge your gestures of extravagance, stop tipping.

I was sitting at a blackjack table a few months ago and was in a hot streak picking up a succession of healthy winning series along the way, making a number of bets for the dealer. Things were going very nicely for a long period of time. A husband and wife came up to play at the table. A few minutes later, the dealer mistakenly called a tie on a hand that I was beaten on.

All of a sudden this woman began screaming at the dealer that he made a mistake. The poor guy turned eight different colors. I didn't say a word. This woman wasn't just making waves, she was intent on creating a typhoon. The dealer tried to appease her, unsuccessfully, and her yelling drew the pit boss over. I couldn't believe how nasty this woman was and I knew my Utopia was over.

Anyhow, the woman made such a fuss that she refused to play with this certain dealer and asked that he be replaced. The pit boss, to quiet her down, excused the dealer and took the shoe himself waiting for the relief dealer. I couldn't believe what happened. On the next hand, the woman broke (she went over 21). I was sitting with a 4, 5, 2, 2, ace & 3, for a six card hand of 17. The dealer had a queen as his up card and turned over an 8. He immediately tapped the table with his knuckle to signify a tie and looked right square at the woman who was doing the yelling. She didn't know whether to cry or lay an egg. She meekly picked up her chips and left the table.

Should you tip? Yes! Rest assured, it won't hurt you!

# ODDS AND ENDS

**4**

## Does Luck Come Into Play?

No! Absolutely, positively NOT. Luck has no place in gambling. I personally do not believe luck will help you at all. I hear people constantly referring to their luck, or lack of same, when discussing their sessions in a casino.

Such statements as:

    a) "Oh, I'm a very lucky person. I win most of the time", or

    b) "Me, I got no luck at all", or

    c) "If luck was a disease, I'd never be sick", or

    d) "I feel lucky today", or

    e) "Man, how can I be so unlucky".

Let me tell you, luck is not going to help you in gambling. Crying about it is just an excuse to make up for the fact that you are probably a rotten player. When you won, it wasn't luck that did it. It was probably good, solid, intelligent play. Or else, the ball just happened to drop into the slot of the number you were playing.

Don't depend on luck, and don't blame it for your failings. If you were a perfect player in the game of your choice you would be aware of the power of knowledge.

Blaming your play on luck is a crutch, and a crutch should only be used when you cannot perform up to your normal capabilities.

# ODDS AND ENDS 5

## Synopsis Of The Big Four

Well, we've come to the crossroads in your approach to gambling. I've explained each facet of the Big Four and given you logical reasons as to why they are all totally dependent on each other. Without all four, you'll have some problem becoming a successful player. By complying with all of the requirments of the Big Four, you will become a strong player, a consistent winner, and most of all, your losses, when they occur, will be tremendously reduced.

1. **BANKROLL.** The amount of money you take to the casino and the starting block for your gambling day. The amount of the bankroll is the sole determining factor for setting your Win Goals and Loss Limits. Without a proper bankroll, which should be 40 times the amount of the table minimum and no less than 30 times the minimum, you cannot and should not gamble.

2. **KNOWLEDGE OF THE GAME.** I don't mean having an idea of the game. I mean being perfect and knowing every possible thing there is to know about your particular choice of game. It won't hurt you to be perfect, and I can't think of a logical reason why you shouldn't be.

3. **MONEY MANAGEMENT.** This is the art of managing that bankroll. What bets you should make after a win and what bets are called for after a loss. It is the art of controlling the money you bring to the casino. Rest assured, if you do not have money management, you in no way, shape, or form have the right to gamble. Ninety-five percent of the people who gamble on anything have no pre-determined method of money control. Don't be counted among that number.

4. **DISCIPLINE.** It is estimated that of all of the people who bet in a casino, approximately 70% of them are ahead at one time or another in accordance with their starting bankroll. But, of that 70%, approximately 90% put back their winnings. Why??? Who knows? Greed, need, stupidity — pick one. My opinion is that it is a total lack of discipline. If you do not have discipline, you're wasting your time even thinking about gambling.

Well, I've touched all the bases. If slots must be played, use my money control system. If you play roulette, pick a system you like and master it. But follow the Big Four.

My phone number, in the event you would like to contact me, is 201-789-3337. Any information about the school and the sports service will be explained upon request.

If you care to write to me, either to discuss the contents of this book or disagree with my theories, feel free to write to me, c/o Gambler, Box 863, Metuchen, NJ 08840.

# ODDS AND ENDS    6

## The Ultimate Goal

Everything I've pointed out to you in this book is aimed at the ultimate goal — winning. You want to follow the rules, I'm proud of you! You want to disagree with me, grab a pen and drop me a line.

I've shown you how to reach the goal, now it is up to you to discipline yourself. The Big Four is the answer. Now is the time to decide if you can handle it. I've covered slots and roulette in this book, but have also published a book on the entire game of blackjack called, naturally, "So You Wanna Be A Gambler" (Blackjack).

If you're interested in a copy, write to me at the address shown. I have also prepared books on craps, card counting, poker and sports.

I sincerely hope you have gained something from these pages and that you will apply my methods to your game of roulette and slots.

The amount that you win is not important. The bottom line is leaving the game you challenge with more money than what you started with. It is possible. All you need is the Big Four and the desire to win.

SO YOU WANNA BE A GAMBLER:

Get the necessary **BANKROLL**.

Absorb all of the **KNOWLEDGE OF THE GAME.**

Learn **MONEY MANAGEMENT.**
Acquire **DISCIPLINE.**
The path leads to success.

Finally, let me leave you with this thought. It is very possible for you to become a consistent winner. Please, please don't play until you learn the game; and then stay within the confines of your starting bankroll.

You will learn to win, and you will love it.

My sincere wishes for success in any endeavor you undertake.

Happy Winnings,
JOHN PATRICK

# SPORTS FORECASTING

## COLLEGE FOOTBALL

## THE PROS: BASEBALL BASKETBALL FOOTBALL

John Patrick's sports picks are given daily
7 Days A Week — 52 Weeks A Year
This service compiled these 1982 figures:

| | |
|---|---|
| **Baseball** | **66% Winners** |
| **Basketball (NBA)** | **64% Winners** |
| **Football (College)** | **65% Winners** |
| **Football (NFL)** | **64% Winners** |

### EACH DAY:
No More Than 3 Picks—Usually Just 1
Handicapping Information For All Members
Selections For The New USFL In 1983

"I would like to talk and meet personally with every person who takes my service. There are different and advanced methods of handicapping, Money Management, and Discipline for Sports Betting."

— John Patrick

# 201-789-3337